SEVEN CRUCIAL MOMENTS

SEVEN CRUCIAL MOMENTS

In Christ's Life
and In Ours

John W. Yates II

MOREHOUSE PUBLISHING
Harrisburg, PA

This book is dedicated to

Alfred Stanway and

John R.W. Stott,

two men of Christ whose influence

upon my life has helped me to

know Christ better, and caused me

to long to give myself to him and to

his purpose.

Acknowledgment
Scripture quotations are from the Revised Standard Version of the Bible, copyright © 1946, 1952, © 1971, 1973 by the Division of Christian Education of the National Council of Churches of Christ in the USA.

Morehouse Publishing
Editorial Office:
871 Ethan Allen Highway
Ridgefield, CT 06877

Corporate Office:
P.O. Box 1321
Harrisburg, PA 17105

Library of Congress Cataloging-in-Publication Data
Yates, John W., 1946-
        Seven crucial moments in Christ's life and in ours / John W. Yates II.
        p.   cm.
        ISBN: 0-8192-1581-3
        1. Jesus Christ—Example.   2. Jesus Christ—Biography.   3. Jesus
Christ—Spiritual life.   I. Title.
BT304.2.Y38 1992   91-44982
232.9'04—dc20   CIP

Printed in the United States of America
by
BSC LITHO
Harrisburg, PA 17105

CONTENTS

FOREWORD

For several years I have been fascinated by the more mysterious moments in the life of Christ which the apostles repeatedly compared to events or developments in the life of the followers of Jesus as well. I have wanted to look at his ascension, for instance, and ask how on earth it could be said that we, too, have in some way been raised to the right hand of God with him, as St. Paul wrote to the Ephesians. The more I have considered these seven moments in the life of Christ, the more deeply aware I have become of the fact that the Holy Spirit has parallel developments to bring about in our own lives. For each of these seven crucial moments in Christ's life—his birth, baptism, temptation, transfiguration, death, resurrection, and ascension—there is a corresponding divine work to be accomplished within his disciples. I hope that this little book of meditations will be helpful to the reader as he or she seeks to come to know Jesus Christ better and become more at one with him in his or her own life. I am particularly grateful to Frank Watson and Suzie Hancock without whose help this book would not have been completed.

John Yates

1

BIRTH

"God comes down that man may rise,
Lifted by him to the skies;
Christ is Son of Man that we
Sons of God in him may be."

Christopher Wordsworth

In the sixth month the angel Gabriel was sent from God to a city of Galilee named Nazareth, to a virgin betrothed to a man whose name was Joseph, of the house of David; and the virgin's name was Mary. And he came to her and said, "Hail, O favored one, the Lord is with you!" But she was greatly troubled at the saying, and considered in her mind what sort of greeting this might be. And the angel said to her, "Do not be afraid, Mary, for you have found favor with God. And behold, you will conceive in your womb and bear a son, and you shall call his name Jesus. He will be great, and will be called the Son of the Most High; and the Lord God will give to him the throne of his father David, and he will reign over the house of Jacob for ever; and of his kingdom there will be no end." And Mary said to the angel, "How shall this be, since I have no husband?" And the angel said to her, "The Holy Spirit will come upon you, and the power of the Most High will overshadow you; therefore the child to be born will be called holy, the Son of God. *(Luke 1:26-35)*

On the wall in my study I have a precious photograph taken in a hospital room a couple of years ago. It's a picture of a young couple from church. He is still wearing the surgical suit that is required in delivery rooms, and she is sitting up in bed. Now, they are clearly worn out and exhausted. Yet there is a joyous sparkle in their faces, an ex-

11

pression of peace, relief, pride, humility, and thankfulness, all rolled up together—because in their arms, wrapped up in white blankets, is a newborn son, weighing eleven pounds, one ounce, and twenty-three inches tall! Nothing in this world was more important to them at that moment than their baby.

That's the way it is when a child is born. Even though I do not know each of you who read this—I could never know everything about your life and what it has been like—I do know that there was a moment in your life when you, too, were the most important person in the world—to many, many people: your mother, your father, your family, the medical people involved who watched and waited and prayed for nine long months, and perhaps much longer. They celebrated and rejoiced that you had come into the world. There is nothing like the birth of a child. Nothing can equal it; nothing should. A baby's birth is God's statement that the human race is worth continuing.

Would the same be true for a child born and then immediately given up for adoption? It would be a little different, but from the relationship I have had with families who have adopted children I would say that their joy is at least as great, or greater, at the coming of that child than the joy of families whose children are naturally their own.

Recently, my mother told my own children the story of the night when their dad was born, and how my father and two older brothers had unexpectedly to transfer some horses that night. They had to ride them in the October moonlight some fifteen miles because of problems on the farm. She told my children of her restlessness and concern as the labor pains began to set in while all of her men were somewhere out there in the darkness, riding horseback, oblivious to the drama that was developing at home.

We never tire of the story of that day or night when we were born. It's our big moment in history, when people laughed, cried, and hugged one another. They celebrated.

They smoked cigars. They drank champagne. They forgot all their problems, at least for a while, just because of our birth. And on our birthday, in some way, we still remember and celebrate that one incredible moment in history when we came into the world.

Once a year, we also celebrate an even more important birth date, that of Jesus. The story of his birth is one story that we never tire of hearing, although we know the details by heart. The account of *your* birth and the story of how *I* was born will soon be all forgotten, but not *history*—because he is the Son of God. In many ways, however, his story is like yours and mine. Mary endured all the discomfort and uncertainty about her unborn child that your mother did, and when he came, it was painful—painful for him, painful for her. He was a helpless infant; he needed to be sheltered, fed, clothed, cleaned, just like all of us.

But from the very beginning, he was clearly different from you and me.

The hymn writer said it so well:

> *Gentle Mary laid her child lowly in a manger;*
>   *There he lay, the undefiled, to the world a stranger...*
> *Angels sang about his birth; wise men sought and found him;*
>   *Heaven's star shown brightly forth, glory all around him.*
> *Shepherds saw the wondrous sight, heard the angels singing;*
>   *All the plains were lit that night, all the hills were ringing...*
> *Son of God, of humble birth, beautiful the story;*
>   *Praise his name in all the earth, hail the king of glory!*

God's own son, born of a virgin. That claim is clear. The authors dare not have made up a tale about that most personal part of the story. Though Mary was his mother, and her body nurtured the seed that became the son, Joseph was not the father. God, by a miracle of holy conception, put his very own seed into the womb of this maiden who had never slept with a man. And, thereby, God entered the human race. Jesus was wholly God and wholly human.

In Trafalgar Square in the middle of London, there stands a tall pillar, and atop that pillar is a statue of Lord Nelson. He is so high up that it is impossible to distinguish any of his features. So several years ago, a new statue, an exact replica of the statue of Nelson, was erected down at eye level, so that everyone could see it close up. This is what God was doing at Christmas—coming down from the height of heaven, so that we might know what he is like at eye level in the person of Jesus.

He was born just as we were born. He lived and grew just as we did, except that at every stage, he showed us how to live. The life he lived was complete. He had no regrets. He had no sins. He lived this earthly life just as you and I do and yet always with a heavenly perspective—he saw things and related to people from the perspective of God his father as well as with the perspective of a first century man. He spoke as God in heaven speaks. And his words are the very words of God. When we look at Jesus' life, we see so much in it that attracts us, don't we?—his wisdom, his power, his consistency, his insight, his genius, his strength, his force of character, his courage, his sense of command, his gentleness, his willingness to sacrifice, his goodness, his holiness, his wholeness.

Jesus is unique. There have been many great men and women throughout history, but only one Jesus. No life has so influenced the world as his. World leaders, famous, outstanding people come and go and their flames burn very brightly—the Roosevelts, the Mikhail Gorbachevs, the Kennedys, the Anwar Sadats—but eventually their flames die down. Not so with Jesus. His flame is still burning as brightly as ever, because he still is, he still lives. We need him, and our lives are incomplete without him. The message of his birth is that we can have him—or, rather, *he* can have *us*. We can be his and he can be ours.

How does it happen? How does the one who is the very Son of God become real in our lives? Before we can understand, we must see first how God was at work at the very beginning; then we come up to the present. In the first chapter of the Bible, we find these words: "In the beginning God created the heavens and the earth. And the earth was formless and void, and darkness was over the surface of the deep; and the Spirit of God was moving over the surface of the waters" (Gen. 1:1,2). The Spirit of God was at work at the very beginning of everything that we know. God's Spirit brought about the creation of all things. Later, the same image that described the work of the Holy Spirit in creation is used by St. Luke speak of God's Spirit coming upon Mary. The Spirit of God *overshadowed* Mary, Luke says, and the Spirit put life in her, the life of Jesus, the very life of God himself. The Holy Spirit in the very beginning had put this same divine life into mankind. The presence of God was alive within man and woman. This is what it means when the Bible says that God created them in his own image, male and female.

And because God was present in their lives, they could know God, walk with God, and talk with God; but the man and the woman turned away from God. They disobeyed God and trampled upon the Spirit of God, and God withdrew his indwelling presence. The Spirit of God no longer filled the human race. God did not take away his love or his concern, but the divine life of God no longer was alive in men and women. People were just people. And people have made a mess of things, haven't they— haven't we? There have been many bright lights, there have been wonderful folks, but by and large, we human beings have squandered our God-given natural resources. We have made selfishness and war the most dominant, recurring themes in world history.

Perhaps that is what the great American statesman Bernard Baruch had in mind years ago, when he was appearing as a witness before a Senate investigative committee. He was asked to suggest what Congress might do to prevent the periodic ups and downs of the nation's economy. And Baruch said, "Pass a law changing human nature and make it retroactive back to the Garden of Eden."

All of us are born naturally selfish, grasping for ourselves and for our own. We see things first and foremost
from our own perspective. And looking out for ourselves is
the most natural thing in the world. It is why, as soon as
wars or revolutions break out, some people go to work
looting the shops and stores, taking and stealing for themselves what they want. This is why we have to have laws,
police, prisons, and armies to preserve the peace and pro-
tect the vulnerable.

We are all as different from Jesus as day is from night.
He is the son of God. We are just people. But that's not the
end of the matter. The rest of the story is this: the same
Holy Spirit who was present at creation and who came
upon Mary, bringing to life the Son of God, is still present
in the world even now. And because of that, we can know
God ourselves and become linked up with God. It is true
that in America, almost everyone says, "Well, certainly I
know God; I talk to God all the time. I believe in Jesus and
God. I pray. I do good things all time." But Jesus said that
unless the same Holy Spirit that came upon Mary comes to
live within a person, that person does not know God and
does not have God's life within them.

Consider a simple example. A couple of summers ago,
my two boys and I bought a lawn mower—a nice lawn
mower—that they use to mow people's lawns during the
summer and earn a little spending money. But it's one of
those lawn mowers that is made to operate on a mixture of
gasoline and oil together. It will operate on gasoline alone,
but if it doesn't have the oil, it is just a matter of time before it burns up. The oil enables it to run as it is intended
to run.

The coming of the Spirit of God into our lives is like
the oil in that machine. God has made us in such a way
that if God's Spirit is living inside us, we live life to the full,
and we live forever. But without Christ in our lives, we
sputter; we never achieve our potential. We eventually

break down altogether. We do the best we can. We eat. We drink. We work. We play. We breathe. We take in information. We process it all. And some do it much better than others. But without the presence of God dwelling in our lives it's like running the mower on gasoline alone. It works for a while, and then it breaks down.

Many people are living just that way. Perhaps you do yourself. St. Paul was praying for some friends: "I fall down on my knees and pray to the Father that out of his glorious, unlimited resources he will give you the mighty inner strengthening of his Holy Spirit. And I pray that Christ will be more and more at home in your hearts, living within you, as you trust in him." Here is how it happens. Jesus said that a change must take place in your life that is every bit as dramatic and as important as your own physical birth. In fact, he said it is like being born, except that whereas our birth was physical, the birth that he makes possible is spiritual.

Perhaps this is what Tennyson had in mind when, frustrated at himself one day, he cried out, "Oh, that a man might arrive in me, that the man I am might cease to be." In a sense, that is what happens to us, although it is not that the person we *are* ceases to be, but that the presence of the Lord Christ comes into our life and helps us become the person we want to be. You see, there is a place inside each of us, the center, that was made for God. And either he has come to dwell there, or someone or something else dwells there. Only you and God know who is there. Many things may dwell there in that central place that is the most important of all. It may be that your family lives there, or your reputation, or your work, or your career. It may be a relationship with another person. It may be pleasure. It may be knowledge. Many things can become gods to us, but only when Christ becomes God to us, and when we give him the first place in our lives, does this open the door and allow the presence of God to come in and dwell in the central place of our lives.

You may have done a good many wonderful things—helped many people, prayed, gone to church, worked tirelessly for good. But if you have made these things ends in themselves, your life is incomplete. You then need to beg God's forgiveness for putting any other thing in the center of your life, and to decide that, above all, you want to be God's man, God's woman, God's daughter, God's son—*and to ask God to take over your life, all of it, lock, stock, and barrel.* God becomes our chief concern—more important than anything or anyone else. Mother Teresa said, "Pray for me that my concern for the poor will not distract me from Jesus Christ." When Christ is at the center of your life, when you take that step and ask him to take that central place, there is a celebration in heaven that is even more wonderful than the celebration that took place when you were born on earth. Jesus told his friends that all the angels in heaven have a party when one single person turns from their own way and gives themselves to God. This is our spiritual birth.

The same angelic host that rejoiced at the Bethlehem birth of Jesus rejoices when you ask him to fill your life with his presence and make you his person. When you were born you did a wonderful thing—you and your mother together. She, through her body, let you know that it was time to be born. And you, tiny little person that you were, said, "O.K." And you were born. God works in the same way with spiritual birth. He lets you know when it's time. He says, "Come to me. Let me take away those things that are in your life that should not be there—that pride, that is not willing to say, 'God, you have your way, I'm number two'; that unwillingness to forgive; that desire to be right; the need to be number one; the relationship that isn't the way it ought to be; those priorities that are all mixed up; that temper; that jealousy; that lust." God says, "Let me take these things away and bring into your life the Spirit of Christ. Believe in me, confess these things, and then let me wash them away and fill you with my presence. I will never leave you, and as you follow me and trust me and obey me, I will begin to make you whole. And what I begin to do in your life here and now, I will complete in you throughout eternity."

Over the last few days, you have probably been concerned with many important things. You have been thinking about loved ones and perhaps about how to honor them. You have been thinking and praying about troubled places around the world. You have thought about the poor, the needy, the homeless. But right at this moment, I just want you to think about yourself and your God. Anything else in life is secondary to that right now. Turning over your life to God, allowing God to fill it with his very own presence is the most important thing you can ever do. Perhaps you have not done this.

Being born is such a simple process. We simply cooperate with our mother. So it is with spiritual birth. We simply cooperate with our heavenly Father. He says to us, "This is the time to let me come into your life and take control." And we say, "Yes. Yes, Lord, I believe, and I give all of myself that I can to all that I know of you."

✣ ✣ ✣ ✣ ✣ ✣ ✣ ✣ ✣ ✣

Reflect on the circumstances of your own birth for a few minutes, giving God thanks for the gift of life and for those who made your birth possible. Have you shared with your closest loved ones the story of your birth? Are there some family members who would benefit from knowing the story better?

For further meditation: Jeremiah 1:4 and 5

Reflective Questions to Ask Myself

1. As I consider my own birth, I also think about this related subject of spiritual birth which Jesus spoke of,
   saying we must be born anew, of the Spirit (John 3).
   Have I myself experienced such a new birth? Has there
   been, in my own life, a period in which I consciously,
   as an act of the will, gave myself as fully as I knew how
   to God, asking Jesus Christ to take full control?

2. If so, now as a maturing Christian, how far has my
   spiritual life progressed? Am I in spiritual infancy?
   adolescence? early maturity? Where do I desire to be
   in my spiritual maturity? Perhaps I should ask God to
   help me in the days ahead, to grow as he would have
   me.

2

BAPTISM

"The sinless one to Jordan came
and in the river shared our stain."

George B. Timms

Then Jesus came from Galilee to the Jordan to John, to
be baptized by him. John would have prevented him,
saying, "I need to be baptized by you, and do you
come to me?" But Jesus answered him, "Let it be so
now; for thus it is fitting for us to fulfil all righteous-
ness." Then he consented. And when Jesus was baptized, he went up immediately from the water, and
behold, the heavens were opened and he saw the
Spirit of God descending like a dove, and alighting on
him; and lo, a voice from heaven, saying, "This is my
beloved Son, with whom I am well pleased." *(Matt.
3:13-17)*

"Could we possibly do this in our neighbor's hot tub?"
a mother asked me the other day, when she was inquiring
about baptism for her daughter. It seemed such a strange
and comical contrast of images to me that I couldn't help
laughing at the idea. A hot tub somehow represents self-
indulgence in the extreme, while baptism symbolizes
something so very different. For a Christian, baptism is
one of those crucial moments. The action itself matters
more than the place or the mode. But why is baptism important to us at all? Looking at Jesus' baptism will help us
to understand our own more clearly. It occurred in the following way.

Most of the crowd that had been close to the river's
edge, listening to the powerful preaching of John the
Baptist and watching whom he baptized in the water, had

now drifted away. John would have been tired and his energy depleted; he was probably resting now, when another came down to him at the river's edge. He was young, strong, vigorous, and all alone. And in his eyes there would have surely been a light such as John had never seen—the light of God was in his face. Jesus had now grown to strong, mature, and magnetic manhood.

"I have come to be baptized too," Jesus said. But John knew instinctively that this was different. The presence of God was in this man, and so John said, "No, that's not right, it is I who should be baptized by you."

"No," said Jesus, "for I must do all things that are right."

And so, there on a quiet bank of the River Jordan, two men went down to the river's edge, and there occurred something so amazing and so profound that the angels in heaven surely must have stared in wonder: a man baptizing the Son of God.

Two high school students at a campus up the road from my house were discussing this very story in the life of Jesus, and one said, "See, this proves Jesus must have been just a normal, sinful man because he needed to be baptized." And the other said, "No, that's not right"—but he wasn't certain why.

Why *was* Jesus baptized? What does it mean? Why are *we* baptized? Well, the answer wasn't clear even to John the Baptist until after the event occurred. There is a good lesson there. Many times you will be shown a step to take or a deed to complete, and you will know inside that this is something you must do, but only later does the reason for it actually become clear.

Jesus had been biding his time in Nazareth, carrying on his father's carpentry business, helping his mother, who was most likely widowed by then, to raise his younger brothers and sisters. He was probably meditating on and pondering the call God had placed on his life since before his birth. Many times when he was young, his parents would have told him the bewildering tale of the angel's visit, the miraculous conception, Joseph's dream, and the marvelous events of that starry night in Bethlehem when the angels sang and the shepherds came.

As the years passed he had learned the scriptures; he had begun to discern some of the mission to which God his Father was calling him. He had found that he could talk with God from the depth of his heart, and the Father in heaven would speak to him. From his earliest youth, he had known God, known God's presence, and probably something of the mystery that they had been one since all eternity. Yet, at the same time, like all of us, he must have had to learn by doing as well. He had to pursue and work at his own relationship with the Father and seek out the meaning and the implications of what it meant to be the Christ. Slowly, gradually, the vision was taking shape.

Meanwhile, his cousin John had left home sooner— perhaps his aged parents, Zechariah and Elizabeth, had already died—and John's incredibly influential ministry was already in full swing. A nationwide spiritual revival had begun. Israel, their nation, had been dry spiritually for centuries—as dry as its barren dust—but all of a sudden, young and old, rich and poor had been stirred, and now, through John, thousands were hungering and longing for spiritual truth and guidance. They were looking for God's light, and John was riding the crest of the wave.

John had done his job, which was to prepare the people for the coming Messiah, and his ministry had brought great encouragement and hope to Jesus. At last, Jesus knew that the time was right, and so he went, at least partly, I think, to be with John and to thank him, to acknowledge his debt to the Baptizer and probably to let John know that now *his* time had come, for John did not know. So when Jesus went to the river, it was at least partly to acknowledge his gratitude to the man whom Jesus called the greatest ever born.

But beyond that, there is a lovelier reason for Jesus'

coming to be baptized. John's ministry was one of warning. John was a man who needed no one and nothing. He had done away with all of life's luxuries and lived on the minimum, caring not the least for popular acclaim or for comfort. He spoke words of judgment—blunt words of rebuke. His hardcutting, condemning, yet crucial words shamed people and made them sorry for their sins. "Repent" was his word, and it is a hard but necessary word, *to* sinners.

Jesus, on the other hand, had a different ministry. While endorsing fully the message of John, Jesus came down to the river at the very beginning of his work to stand *beside* sinners. He who was without sin came to demonstrate the all-encompassing love of God for the sinner. And Jesus going down to be baptized, you see, was really a picture of God coming down to call and save us.

In the coming days, people would say of Jesus, "He's the friend of sinners." Isaiah said, "A bruised reed he would not break." He went where society's outcasts were, to the tables of the treacherous and traitorous, and talked with those whose lives were full of shame. Isaiah had predicted that the Messiah would be "numbered with the transgressors," and so it was. Here in the Jordan River, Jesus was saying, "I have come to stand by the side of the one who knows he has sinned and is sorry; the one who is in trouble and knows she needs help; the one who is sick and longs for healing; the one who is tired and needs rest." Jesus' baptism was his first step—the first of a multitude of difficult steps, the final one of which was when he embraced death on the cross.

Jesus came, then, to be baptized for three reasons: *one*, to show his gratitude to John; *two*, to identify with all people; and *three*, to begin his life's work with John's support and with the full endorsement of his heavenly Father, and to be fully empowered for it by the Holy Spirit. For in order to complete his task, he would need all the power of heaven—he would need the fullness of the Holy Spirit which he received. But it is the second reason for his baptism—to identify with humanity—that I want you to ponder for just a moment more.

I know a man who was so derelict in his duty, so irresponsible, that his wife could not hold back her words of wrath. Her indignation that he could have been so immature and thoughtless—even though he had been made well aware of the harm that would befall his family should he fail—was totally justified, and so were her words of judgment.

The man had been a fool! And when she exploded, then he realized this and was filled with remorse. He needed that John-the-Baptist type of denunciation. He needed to see and repent of his foolhardiness. And yet he needed more. He also needed someone to come down and stand beside him and say, "I am with you, yet." He needed someone to say, "I forgive you in spite of your sin. Turn from it now, make restitution as best as you can, begin again." This is what God did in Christ! This is the major reason why Jesus was baptized.

Did you know that at its deepest meaning, the word "baptism" means to be fully and completely identified with? It does not just mean to dip or immerse or sprinkle but to absorb, to envelop and to fully enter into the feelings and ideas of another.[1] This is what Jesus was doing throughout his entire ministry. He was entering into our life so that he, the Son of God, could identify with us.

"He had to become like us in all things," the writer to the Hebrews said, "so that he could be our merciful and faithful High Priest before God, a priest who would be both merciful to us and faithful to God in dealing with the sins of the people" (Heb. 2:17).

Take a handkerchief, a nice white, clean, linen handkerchief, and immerse it in a goblet of wine—hearty red, Burgundy wine—and what happens? The white handkerchief becomes fully identified with the wine as it absorbs it. When Jesus stepped into the Jordan River, it was his first official step as a grown man, into the goblet of our life—our ills, our hurts, our burdens, our sins. It was like being dipped in the wine, and the pure white Lamb of God was becoming drenched in the blood-red sins of the human race. Thus John with prophetic vision, remembering perhaps the words of Isaiah 1:18, "Though your sins be as scarlet they shall be washed as white as snow," soon proclaimed this to the masses—introducing Jesus to them, saying, "Behold, the Lamb of God who comes to take away the sins of the world."

This is why Jesus was baptized—to become one of us. But should we not also ask, "What about us?" Why are we baptized here, two thousand years later, in a very different place and culture? There are three simple reasons why we are baptized. *First*, Jesus commanded it—in Matthew 28:19, "Go and make disciples, baptizing them in the name of the Father and the Son and the Holy Spirit," and in Mark 16:16, "He who has believed and has been baptized shall be saved, but he who has disbelieved shall be condemned." It pleases God when we are baptized. It publicly demonstrates our love for him. That is the first reason: Jesus commanded it.

Secondly, we are baptized in order to be identified with Jesus. Remember that the word "baptize" means to become fully identified with—to become one with. It is an outward action that we take to signify something that happens inside of us. That is what a sacrament is. It is much more than just a ceremony. Baptism is our way of showing that we accept Jesus as the one who makes it possible for our sins to be forgiven. When he was baptized, he took our sin upon himself. When we are baptized we are taking his goodness upon ourselves. He became scarlet, we become pure white.

Think for a moment of a gold wedding ring that symbolizes marriage. In somewhat the same way, baptism symbolizes our marriage to Christ, our new life with him. Now the ring does not *make* you married, nor does baptism *make* you a Christian, but if a person doesn't have the ring, it is pretty safe to assume that he or she is not married, and since New Testament times if a person was not baptized, you could almost assume they were not believers.

My wife and I were good friends for years. Then that friendship became love. We made a commitment to each other, and we were married. I gave her a gold ring and she took my name. Miss Alexander became Susan Alexander Yates—Mrs. Yates. She then had a new identity and a new role, as did I. We were no longer single, we were now two—two who had become one. Many things began to change, then, because of our new identity.

In baptism, we come to Christ as a bride comes to her husband. We come as sinners and we become forgiven Christians. We are married to Christ, and our identity is changed through our commitment to him and his commitment to us! Just as in marriage. When an adult is baptized, this commitment to Christ is made and we celebrate it! When an infant is baptized the child's commitment to Christ is yet to come—we prayerfully anticipate it! So baptism is identification with Christ, taking his name, as in a wedding.

A *third* thing that happens in baptism, a third reason why we are baptized, is that it signifies new ownership. To the west of Washington, D.C., out in the Shenandoah Mountains is a town to which I sometimes go. In that town is an old diner covered with graffiti and not known for its cleanliness. I go there for the atmosphere, which is hard to find here in Washington! Above the diner is a large sign that says, "Nick's Diner." This sign has greeted generations, proclaiming that the diner is owned by Nick. Similarly, *baptism* is the sign that says that a person belongs to God. Baptism does not *make* a person belong to God, any more than Nick's sign *makes* him the owner of the store. It is just an indicator—a mark of ownership—that shows that a transaction has been made. St. Paul said, "You are no longer your own, you belong to Christ." Baptism is the sign that tells this to the world.

Baptism is a precious gift. We must cling to it and
honor it. It reminds us that we are God's. It is said of
Martin Luther, that great and mighty man of God who
turned the church on its ear five hundred years ago, that
he had moments, even hours, when he seemed to be totally confused about everything. For nearly thirty years, he
was in the forefront of a spiritual revolution which un-
doubtedly produced great strain and exhaustion—mental,
physical, and spiritual (much as we would expect to be
true of someone like Lech Walesa today, in the vanguard of
revolution). Luther had times when he questioned everything—the faith, the value of the Reformation, even the
scriptures—but at those times, we are told, he would write
with chalk in bold letters on his table, *Baptizatus sum*—"I
am baptized." This reassured him that he did in truth belong to God, and eventually he got moving again. I have
been baptized, I am God's, and therefore, nothing else really matters.

Sometimes life becomes so very hard that we just feel
we want to give up. A woman told a little story about her
son, Jason: "When he was seven, I sent him off to school
one day, and a little while later there was a knock at the
door, and I opened the door and it was Jason. I asked,
'Jason, what are you doing here?' He said, 'I've quit school.'
'Why have you quit school?' I asked. 'Well, it was too long,
it was too hard and it was too boring,' he answered. I said,
'Jason, you have just described life, get back on the bus!'"

Sometimes we are like young Jason. When you feel
that you, too, want to quit, I want to urge you to remember Jesus' baptism, and that he stands beside you.
Remember Luther, in all his frustration and confusion, saying, "I am baptized," and remind yourself as well: "I belong to him, and that is enough. I, too, can get back on the
bus and keep going."

In Jesus' baptism, he has become one of us. In our baptism, we become one of his. He is ours, we are his.

Assuming that you, the reader, have been baptized, what do you know of your baptism, the date, the place, the persons present, the things going on in the world at that time? If you do not know the answer to these questions you might be interested to find out. It should not be that difficult. If you do know, are there loved ones who would like to know this story. If you were not baptized, is it time for you to take this step now?

For further meditation: Mark 16:16, Acts 2:38, Acts 8:12

Reflective Questions to Ask Myself

1. Have I really understood that Jesus came to be the "friend of sinners"? When I disobey God do I turn to Jesus as a friend, or turn away from him in my selfishness or shame? Why?

2. In my relationships with others am I more like John the Baptist, pronouncing judgment, or like Jesus, offering forgiveness?

3. How does belonging to Jesus Christ affect my life today?

3

TEMPTATION

"No man knows how bad he is until he has
tried to be good. There is a silly idea about
that good people don't know what temptation means."

C.S. Lewis

"My temptations have been my masters in divinity."

Martin Luther

Then Jesus was led up by the Spirit into the wilderness to be tempted by the devil. And he fasted forty
days and forty nights, and afterward he was hungry.
And the tempter came and said to him, "If you are the
Son of God, command these stones to becomes loaves
of bread." But he answered, "It is written, 'Man shall
not live by bread alone, but by every word that pro-
ceeds from the mouth of God.'" Then the devil took
him to the holy city, and set him on the pinnacle of
the temple, and said to him, "If you are the Son of
God, throw yourself down; for it is written, 'He will
give his angels charge of you,' and 'On their hands
they will bear you up, lest you strike your foot against
a stone.'" Jesus said to him, "Again it is written, 'You
shall not tempt the Lord your God.'" Again, the devil
took him to a very high mountain, and showed him all
the kingdoms of the world and the glory of them; and
he said to him, "All these I will give you, if you will
fall down and worship me." Then Jesus said to him,
"Begone, Satan! for it is written, 'You shall worship
the Lord your God and him only shall you serve.'"
Then the devil left him, and behold, angels came and
ministered to him. (*Matt. 4:1-11*)

No American leader has had to face tougher problems
or had to deal with less grateful people than George

Washington did, first as Commander-in-Chief of the Colonial troops and then as President. His entire career involved one extreme test after another. The thing that impresses me most about him is not what a great and indispensable man he was, but that he always resisted the temptation to throw in the towel and go home to Mount Vernon. He loved nothing so dearly as he loved his farm, and he wanted nothing so strongly as he wanted to be there with his family, living as a farmer. But Washington was a marked man. He was the man who could rally the country, who could unite the colonies and inspire the troops. He was the only man of his day who could really hold the ship of state on course and lead this young nation. That was the work to which God called him. That was his duty, and he did not shirk it. He did not seek it, for he wanted to avoid the sacrifice involved; but he did what he had to do for his country.

And in facing all these tests one after the other, head on, doing the best he could, seeking the help of God, he became the father of this country. What he wanted was to retire to Mount Vernon. What he committed himself to, however, was one difficult task after another. The result was a secure and successful beginning for the nation, and in the process, Washington grew into true greatness.

This is a principle which we all must come to understand. Testing is vitally important, because it shows what a person is made of. And in the most difficult, testing times, the true strength and greatness of a person is revealed. You wouldn't buy an automobile or a television set that had not been fully tested and proven to be reliable. The testing shows what a thing is really made of. But *beyond* that, the testing itself helps us actually to become stronger ourselves.

We read in scripture about the testing or the temptation of Jesus. This story of his testing in the wilderness is one of the most personal and private times in the life of the Lord. We only know about that time because he later shared it with the Twelve. He was completely alone when this event occurred, and in telling the story later on, the Lord was laying bare his own soul to the disciples, telling about a time of agonizing and temptation through which he had come, so that out of *his* struggles, his disciples might be helped in *their* struggles.

Remember, that at this time in his life, Jesus had just experienced an amazing mountaintop experience. He was thirty years old, and up until that time he had maintained a completely private life. He had not been in the public eye at all. He then submitted himself to his cousin, John the Baptist, to be baptized, and in the midst of that, as he came up from the shallow waters on the banks of the Jordan River, the heavens opened up, the Spirit of God came down upon him, and the voice of God spoke from heaven announcing that this was God's son, the long awaited Messiah.

No person had ever had such an experience, and it confirmed to Jesus that God's purpose for his life was to lead people back to God, to be "the way, the truth, and the life." But the gospels then tell us that at that moment the Holy Spirit immediately compelled the Lord to go out into the wilderness to be alone, and ultimately to undergo a time of testing and temptation.

It is often true that high points in our lives are immediately followed by times of difficulty and times of testing. Have you noticed that sometimes, just when you think you are at your strongest, you fail? Just when you think you've learned how to be a wise parent, for instance, you blow it. Just after a basketball team plays its heart out and wins the victory in the toughest game of the season, it loses to Podunk College. Sometimes this is true in the spiritual realm as well. Sometimes it happens that we have a beautiful spiritual experience with God. We are greatly inspired, we seem to have reached a new level of Christian maturity, and then the very next day, we fall into deep depression or commit some thoughtless or shameful deed that we thought we had long since overcome. So often the

great moments are followed by very difficult moments.
This is what happened to Christ.

He was faced at this moment in his life with the question of how he would carry out his work. What would be his method of bringing people back to God? He decided to be completely alone with God and, through fasting and prayer, to seek guidance from his Father in heaven. He went out into the wilderness, an area known to the Jews as The Devastation. Here Jesus could be completely free to think. His was the most important mission any person had ever had, and the most difficult. No one could help him with his decision; it could only be determined by himself alone with his heavenly Father's help.

How difficult it is for some of us to get completely alone. Some do not understand the need for solitude, and those who do are too seldom able to gain it. There are times when we *must* get away from everyone, away from all noises and distractions, away from all actions, from everyone else's advice, simply to think and pray. It may be that some big mistakes would be avoided if we would simply take time to be alone. Solitude is vital. But in *his* solitude, the Lord was tempted and tested.

What is Temptation?

What is temptation? In the Bible it takes many forms, but basically we understand temptation in two different ways. We are tempted, first of all, by a seductive power to depart from God's ways. The other type of temptation is a trial or a testing or a proving which God seems to allow us to experience, not only to see what stuff we are made of and how strong our faith is, but also to see whether we are faithful to God *through* the time of testing. And if we are faithful, this also helps us to learn more about God's faithfulness to us when we are in need.

God knew what lay ahead for Jesus, but Jesus, at this time, probably did *not* know. His commitment to his

Father's will had to be tested. He had to undergo an experience which would dramatically solidify his strength of purpose, if he was to be able successfully to overcome all the coming trials and the temptations to avoid the cross. And so, this time of thinking and planning became a time of severe testing as well. It had to be that way.

Does God still allow his children to be tested? Yes. Why? First, to ascertain our faithfulness to him. He has heard our prayers, our claims. Now he will see what we are really made of—he will prove us. Secondly, *we* need to discern what we are made of, as well.

In times of testing, we can grow and make great gains. When I was sixteen, I was in an extremely difficult French class. My professor was impatient and incredibly demanding—at least I thought he was. My grades were poor, to say the least, and I can still remember getting back homework papers that had so much red ink on them that I was afraid someone else would see them. Once he had apparently given up correcting a homework paper in disgust, halfway through, and made a rip in the page with his red pen! I wanted to quit. It didn't seem worth it to me, but a little voice inside (not to mention a louder voice from my parents) seemed to say, "Persevere, you can do it." My grade hovered around the passing level, and I approached the final exam with genuine fear and trembling. Days after the exam was over, when the grades were posted, I was on my way to look at the board and see whether I had passed or failed. Just as I rounded the corner, I bumped into my professor who looked at me and said, "Well, Yates, I see from your exam grades that at last you have demonstrated what you are capable of." I was so thrilled I would have fallen down and kissed his feet. I had made an 89—an unheard of grade for me. I learned through that time of difficulty that I could grow and make great gains. Trials can reveal our hidden strengths.

Then, also, times of trials enable us to experience the reality of God's goodness in a deeper way, if we will. In times of great difficulty, we find God to be so much greater than we ever knew. Forty percent of Americans who said that their faith has significantly changed explain that this change came about in times of great turbulence.

When our circumstances are prosperous, it is easy to forget and to live without God. And so, for that reason, just as an eagle stirs up the nest and forces her young ones out into midair—so that they must, of necessity, use their wings—so God allows us to be tossed about by troubles so that we might grow up.

If you want to fly a kite, you must take the string and run until the kite rises into the heavens. It will not fly if there is no wind. The wind is necessary in order to fly kites, and they rise, interestingly, not with the wind, but against it. Something similar is true for us as we encounter trials. We will not achieve maturity unless we surmount trials and difficulties.

When the Confederate army retreated after Gettysburg, General Lee wrote Jefferson Davis a letter in which he made this remarkable statement: "We must expect reverses, even defeats. They are sent to teach us wisdom and prudence, to call forth greater energies, and to prevent our falling into greater disasters."

A man happened to meet his minister on the street one day and in conversation told him of all the difficulties and troubles he had had during the last year. He concluded by saying, "I tell you right now, preacher, it's enough to make a man lose his religion." To which the minister responded, "It's enough to make a man *use* his religion, I would say." Phillips Brooks said, "O, do not pray for easy lives. Pray to be stronger men. Do not pray for tasks equal to your powers. Pray for powers equal to your tasks."

I know that some of you right now face very difficult situations—some feel disheartened, discouraged, overwhelmed. I do not know if your problem is from God or from Satan, but I do know God wants to see you *through* it and past it and to strengthen you in it.

Now, keeping this in mind, let us return and look at Jesus' own experience. The Judean desert is a hot and foreboding place. It's dry. There is little vegetation most of the year. There is very little to eat, and not a lot to drink. Jesus was tired, hungry, and thirsty. He may even have been struggling with fear. And when we are tired, and when we have needs and are faced with quite a difficult challenge or choice, we are prime candidates for temptation. So the tempter confronted Jesus with three ideas about how to be a successful Messiah—how to gain the loyalty of the people to whom he was coming. First, the temptation was, "Use the power that God has given you to turn stones to bread. Feed the people. Become a great humanitarian worker. Give the people everything they want to satisfy their hunger, and then you will have those people literally eating out of your hand. Everybody will follow you." This wasn't the kind of allegiance Jesus wanted.

Then the thought came, "Worship Satan as the prince of this world." And if he would do that, then the promise was that he could have the whole world as his kingdom. If he would use the devil's methods, weapons of force, cruelty, and ruthlessness, then instead of winning people's hearts by self-sacrifice and suffering, he could force them to follow him. That was not acceptable to the Lord either.

Then the final temptation was just to be a wonder-worker and use his miracles to attract people to follow him. This thought came to his mind: "You don't want to begin your ministry just by going and being baptized in that little muddy stream by that fellow John the Baptist. Do something spectacular. Stand atop the temple of Mount Zion, at the corner where there is a 450-foot drop from the pinnacle down to the ground in the Valley of Kidron below."

The Jews had a tradition that when the Messiah came, he would appear, as it were, out of heaven. And he would stand on the pinnacle of the temple and announce publicly his claim to be the king of the Jews. So the devil said,

"Why don't you do that, and then leap out into space? And since you are the Son of God, you will land unhurt. Overwhelm all those people and they will follow you like flies after honey."

These were the three temptations—temptations to turn away from God's ways and embrace the ways of the world. "You can't trust that God's way will work in the end...look, you don't have to call people to repentance, just feed them, give people what they want, it's so much easier...compromise your standards a little bit, ease up."

The devil even quoted—or misquoted—from scripture. He took a passage out of context (Psalm 91). He twisted it to his own advantage. But Jesus knew that this thinking was unacceptable, and he answered the tempter, "It is written, 'You shall not tempt the Lord your God.'"

When We Tempt God

Consider that thought for a moment: "You shall not tempt the Lord your God." Jesus was using a quote from the Old Testament, the book of Deuteronomy 6:16, to say something profound about temptation—that it is possible for us to tempt God as well as for us to be tempted. What does this mean? It means that we try to see how far we can push God to fulfill our own desires. To do what the tempter suggested would have been to expect God to help us when we pursue what we want, rather than what God wants. That, says Jesus, is to tempt God.

We tempt God when we wilfully disobey God. We tempt God when we expect God to help us as we selfishly pursue our own way rather than God's way. We tempt God when we look for God's miracles to intervene and save us from the consequences of our foolishness. We tempt God when we consciously put ourselves into a dangerous position to which God has not in any way called us. We tempt God when we consciously disobey God and then ask him to help us while we are still in a state of disobedience. We tempt God when we ask him to help us, but we have not used the natural, ordinary means that God has given us to escape danger or to accomplish our God-given objectives. We tempt God sometimes, I fear, when we expect God to work a miracle just to satisfy our impatience. God does not often bless us when we seek to take shortcuts in accomplishing his purposes.

A teenager who had not done her homework was about to take a test. So she prayed, "Oh, God, let someone sit next to me who knows the answers so that I can do well on this test." That's tempting God. A man who leaves his wife and moves in with another woman, when confronted, says, "It can't be wrong because it feels so good." That's tempting God.

But there is another related way in which we tempt God, and this, too, was Jesus' temptation. This is through doubting God. It is through not trusting God to keep his word. It is doubting his presence, doubting his faithfulness to us. Over and over we find examples of this in the Bible and in our own lives. God allowed his people to endure very difficult times and they were tempted to believe that God no longer cared, that God was no longer in control. The truth was that God was in control, but he *was seeking to strengthen their confidence in him.* God always allows us to be tested so that we can learn to live by faith in his promises. That is how we learn to walk by faith. Faith does not grow in easy times, it grows in the desert—in hard times. When you do not have what you need, it can either threaten your faith or it can strengthen it.

To tempt God means to doubt God's care for us, to question his faithfulness; it means impatient unbelief in the God who is there and the God who cares. Here is a spiritual principle. God has made certain promises. For example, God has promised to be with us for ever and ever. God has promised to guide us and to meet our needs. God has promised to see us through this life and bring us safely into the next. But to grumble and be skeptical of these promises, to complain or to make demands upon God, is unbelief and presumption—and that is how we tempt God. It may be natural, but it is not acceptable to God.

All of us have times of doubt, times when we just don't believe. Many of us have serious needs. You may have lost a mate or a marriage. You may have lost a job or material security. You may be feeling all alone. You may be without any friends. You may feel as though you are drying up on the inside and have great needs, and no one seems to know what your needs are. And God seems so very far away from you. You may feel that your prayers aren't being answered. You may feel angry with God. You may feel frustrated with God. You may have had sadness piled upon sadness, until you feel that you are at the breaking point.

God did not promise to keep us out of the desert. He only promised to be with us there. It is not evil to have these moments of doubt. The tempter comes, and he whispers in our ear, "Doubt. Question. Grumble." It is not wrong to be tempted. It is wrong to give in to the temptation. The enemy plants the seed of doubt, but unless we water it, it won't grow. When you feel yourself being overcome by a spirit of doubt, or complaining, or when you are becoming angry with God, let me recommend that, first of all, you talk honestly to God about your feelings. Then talk to a close, believing friend, pour your heart out to that person, and let that person comfort you, encourage you, and pray for you. Then, take time to thank God for the ways in which he has blessed you and provided for you every step of the way thus far. Praise God and ask him to replace your doubt with peace.

Two Promises

Finally, remember two precious promises which are good news that never grows old. These two promises hold true in the face of all kinds of trials and temptations. The first: "God causes all things to work together for good to those who love the Lord and are called according to his purposes" (Rom. 8:28). Note that this promise of "all things working together" is like the ingredients of a cake being mixed together. Some taste good by themselves, but such things as baking powder, flour and alum do not. However, they are essential to the final product and, blended together by skilled hands, produce a delicious dessert. God can be trusted to take even the bitter experiences of life and blend them together and make them "work together for good." God knows they are needed ingredients, and, as the Master Chef, he knows they can produce the desired results.

The second promise: "No temptation has seized you except what is common to man, and God is faithful, he will not let you be tempted beyond what you can bear, but when you are tempted, he will also provide a way out so that you can stand up under it" (1 Cor. 10:13). This is a crucial principle to remember. When airlines train their pilots, they first do so by the use of a simulator. The simulator is designed to present the pilot with a variety of problems, so that he will be able to handle any emergency in the future. They start by testing the pilot with simple problems, and then they build up to catastrophic situations. They never test the pilots beyond their abilities, but slowly give them more difficult problems when they have mastered the previous ones. These pilots, upon completing their courses, are fully prepared, mature pilots, ready to handle any problem that comes their way. This is similar to God's method of working with us, teaching us how to handle the problems of life. God never gives us more than we can handle, but teaches us through our trials so that we can be fully equipped, mature people, ready to handle any problem of life that might come our way.

Henry Ward Beecher, a preacher in the nineteenth century, said, "No physician ever weighed out medicine for his patients with half so much care and exactness as God weighs out to us every trial. Not one gram too much does he ever permit to be put on the scale."

If Jesus, in all his maturity, was tempted to doubt or disobey God, certainly we will be also. If you are not now in a time of testing, you will be. See it for what it is, an opportunity to grow. It can make you bitter or make you better. Sometimes it is difficult to believe and to obey, and we all fail. But the Christ who withstood the temptation is the Christ who lives in you, and he will see you through as you look to him.

Whereas birth and baptism are momentary events, temptation is a process that sometimes is momentary but often lasts a long time, particularly when we understand temptation as a testing or trying time. We tend to view these times negatively, but can you recall instances of trial in your own life that actually resulted in your own maturing or strengthening? Do you have children, parents, relatives or friends who might benefit from hearing about those times of trial in your own past?

For further meditation: Hebrews 4:14-16

Reflective Questions to Ask Myself

1. Am I aware of a temptation in my own life right now? to disobey God? to rationalize something in my life? to run away from a thing I am being led to do? to impatiently doubt God? to question his faithfulness? to complain? to be anxious? to condemn or harm another?

2. How important is it to me to be faithful to God in all areas of my life? Am I facing my temptation in a way that demonstrates my desire to please God?

3. Do I want an easier life or to become a stronger person?

4

TRANSFIGURATION

"O wondrous type! O vision fair
of glory that the Church may share,
which Christ upon the mountain shows,
where brighter than the sun he glows!"

John Mason Neale

Now about eight days after these sayings he took with
him Peter and John and James, and went up on the
mountain to pray. And as he was praying, the appearance of his countenance was altered, and his raiment
became dazzling white. And behold, two men talked
with him, Moses and Elijah, who appeared in glory
and spoke of his departure, which he was to accomplish at Jerusalem. Now Peter and those who were
with him were heavy with sleep, and when they wak-
ened they saw his glory and the two men who stood
with him. And as the men were parting from him,
Peter said to Jesus, "Master it is well that we are here;
let us make three booths, one for you and one for
Moses and one for Elijah"—not knowing what he said.
As he said this, a cloud came and overshadowed them;
and they were afraid as they entered the cloud. And a
voice came out of the cloud, saying, "This is my Son,
my Chosen; listen to him!" And when the voice had
spoken, Jesus was found alone. And they kept silence
and told no one in those days anything of what they
had seen. *(Luke 9:28-36)*

When he was a young man, John D. Rockefeller was
strong and healthy. He determined to make all the money
he could and drove himself relentlessly to the very limit of
his abilities. He had earned his first million by the age of
thirty-three. Within ten years, he controlled the biggest

company in the world. At age fifty-three he was the wealthiest man on earth—the world's only billionaire.

At that moment in his life, however, he suddenly developed a strange sickness called alopecia. He lost all his hair, eyelashes, and eyebrows. His entire body became shrunken and wrinkled. He could only manage to digest milk and crackers. He was not loved by people. In fact, he found it necessary to have bodyguards. His life became miserable. He could not sleep, he stopped smiling, and enjoyed nothing in life.

His physician predicted that he would not live more than a year or so, and, in fact, the newspapers had already written his obituary in advance to be used whenever he died. In the process of those sleepless nights, he began to think about things other than money. He realized he "could not take one dime" into the next world. Some things were more important than money.

Suddenly, he became a different person. He began to help churches with his wealth and began to get involved in caring for the poor. He established the Rockefeller Foundation, which made possible countless wonderful philanthropic actions, including the medical research that led to the discovery of penicillin and other drugs. Rockefeller began to be able to sleep again and to eat and enjoy life. It had been thought that he would not live beyond fifty-four, but he lived to be ninety-eight years old.

People can change. People *do* change. Christ knew this and taught it over and over again. But he also underwent an experience that demonstrated this truth in a remarkable way.

While much of the life of Jesus was unusual and unique, the event that we call the transfiguration is truly remarkable. Three of the four gospels tell this story—each gospel writer adding his own little insights. Two of the men who were on the mountain top with Jesus—the third died shortly after the resurrection—wrote about this experience and described it as perhaps the most remarkable of all the things that they saw in the three years that they were with Jesus. It was toward the end of his three-year public ministry. Jesus had come to the terrible conclusion that God wanted him to die—to suffer, to be crucified, and to die. He had told his friends this but was still wrestling with it. And he wanted to be sure that his recent decision to go to Jerusalem, where he knew he would face arrest, was right. So he went up into the mountains, way to the north of Israel, probably on the slopes of Mount Hermon (today Lebanon), to be still and to ask his Father, "Am I doing what you want by deciding to return to Jerusalem?"—because he knew it meant the end. He wanted to listen to God's voice to be sure.

Jesus only had one concern in life, and that was to do the Father's will. So he went to pray, that he might better know God's will, and he took along Peter and James and John to be with him. There, on the slopes of that mountain, three things happened. First, he underwent a remarkable physical experience. His whole being changed in appearance. Second, Moses and Elijah came back from the dead and spoke with him. Third, God himself overshadowed all of them and spoke out of the clouds—three amazing things all at once.

First, he was *transfigured,* the Bible says:

> And he was transfigured before them, and his face shone like the sun, and his garments became white as light. (Matt. 17:2)

His whole person was suffused with a bright, white light. In the gospel bearing his name, Mark wrote that Jesus' clothes were whiter than any launderer would ever be able to bleach them. His face and his clothes glistened—bright, says St. Luke, bright as a flash of lightning. But the startling thing is that in this account of this event, the writer carefully uses a word to make it clear to those of us who were not there that the light did not come from above or behind or beyond. In other words, God did not unleash a lightning bolt as a bright spotlight shining on his Son. No, the word that is used specifically tells us that the light was from within the man himself. In other words, all of the dazzling glory and brightness of God himself that was in Jesus but had been hidden by his earthly body since he left his throne in heaven, was now, for just a few moments, revealed and released. Those who were there saw something of the actual glory of God and of heaven. John, in the first chapter of his gospel, said, "We beheld his glory, glory as of the only Son from the Father." Peter, the other one who wrote of this, said, "We were eyewitnesses of his majesty, his splendor, his glory."

Some time ago, I saw a wonderful movie entitled *Glory,* about the heroic all Black 54th Massachusetts Infantry Regiment in the Civil War. It is a movie about glory, but the glory that this movie presents is a different sort from the glory that we are seeing here on the mountain. The movie shows what can happen to a group of downtrodden, mostly illiterate folks. who commit themselves to a noble vision and endure great hardship and condescension because of their determination to spend themselves in the cause of freedom. Through dogged determination, discipline, perseverance, persistence, dependence on one another, and dependence upon God, they also become strong. They become inspirational examples of moral courage, and in the process, they become men, in every sense of the word—great men. And in that is a sense of wonder and glory. It is a glorious chapter in the history of our nation.

The glory of Jesus was all of this, but much more. It was the radiance of God within Jesus, hidden for thirty-three years, but now, for just a few moments, revealed. He was gleaming, his whole being was pulsating with light, an inner light. And it was so frightening and so unexpected that Peter became incoherent. He is described as babbling uncontrollably. One of the gospel writers says that Peter really did not know what he was saying. And John says later, in the book of Revelation, that when he saw the glory of Jesus he fainted dead away. They both fell to the ground!

That is the first thing that happened. The second, equally remarkable, is the appearance of Moses and Elijah. Matthew 17:3 tells us, "Behold, there appeared to them Moses and Elijah, talking with him." Luke adds that these two men—two great heroes of the Old Testament, who themselves had had remarkable face-to-face encounters with the living God on sacred mountain tops and had been mysteriously taken away by God at the end of their lives— came and spoke with Jesus about his own departure, his exodus, his leaving for Jerusalem. Here, then, were the greatest lawgiver and a great prophet, each of whom had been called by God in his own day to set out on remark- able journeys without knowing exactly what would befall him, and who had found God to be utterly reliable in showing them the way and providing for him. These two came now to Jesus, sent by the Father to reassure the Son that he was doing what the Father wanted. I like to think that perhaps, as Moses was talking, he was reminding Jesus about how God had guided him, Moses, years be- fore—recounting the story about the fire by night and the cloud by day that led the children of Israel out from Egypt to the Promised Land.

Is this story difficult for us to believe? Yes, but perhaps it should not seem so strange. Integral to our own Christian faith is the conviction of life beyond death. Heaven is just beyond our own frail sight, it is just on the "other side" of this physical world that we perceive. Is it all that unusual to believe that, from time to time, God might pull back the curtain slightly and allow a peek into the larger life beyond? This is what happened. For a few moments, two persons who had already passed through the doorway of death into the next life were allowed to step back into time and converse with God's Son. It was not the first time this had happened, nor would it be the last.

Perhaps Moses was reminding Jesus about God's guid-
ing with the cloud when the third unusual thing happened. The same cloud, the bright and luminous cloud
that had always represented the very presence of God, settled over them on the top of the mountain. It is not unusual for clouds to be around mountain tops. It happens
all the time. It happens on Mount Hermon. And, at first,
no one would have thought anything of it; a fog was coming in. But then evidently the cloud began to glow, and
they heard a voice speak from within the cloud: "'This is
my beloved Son, with whom I am well pleased; listen to
him.' When the disciples heard this, they fell on their
faces" (Matt.17:5-6). They all knew they were in the presence of Jehovah God who spoke to reassure his Son and to
reassure them as well. Just writing the story was evidently,
for St. Matthew, such a powerful, moving experience that
in this paragraph, although you don't really notice it, three
different times he stops and interjects a little Greek word
that is often omitted but understood. It is variously trans-
lated "Look!" or "Behold!" It is really just a particle, and
what it means is, "Now, wait a minute!" or "Don't miss
this!" or "This is incredible!" You know that when you are
telling a story and trying to build up suspense, you say,
"Now, look!" or "Listen!" or "Let me tell you." Three times
he uses that expression in this one paragraph. It is almost
as though he caught his breath at the sheer incredibility of
what was happening.

For just a moment, they caught a glimpse of the glory
of heaven. Moses had seen it before. He had seen it on
Mount Sinai. Isaiah had seen it in the Temple. The book of
Revelation says that the holy city in heaven has no need
for a sun or a moon, because this same glory of God is
everywhere present.

When we read such an incredible story, we ask, "Why
did this happen?" I have come to at least three conclusions
as to why it happened.

First, it must have been God's way of confirming to

Jesus that he was, indeed, moving in the right direction. His decision to give his life as a sacrifice for the sin of the world was the right thing. And, second, this was God's way of encouraging the disciples to stay with Jesus, to believe in him, to go to the end with him, and to listen closely to his words. Surely an experience like this would show them that whatever happened on Good Friday, God was in Christ, and Christ was fulfilling God's purposes. But the third reason, I think, is that there is a message in this for us. There is always a message for us in the crisis moments of the life of Christ, and this is the message here: just as Jesus experienced a transfiguration, God wants you to be transfigured as well.

Our Own Transfiguration

Our transfiguration is not quite like that of Jesus, but it's just as real and just as breathtaking if we can grasp what it's about. Now, this is not my idea. This is a truth that is repeated over and over again in scripture, but it is one we are likely to skip over, because we don't understand or we forget. But the fact is that the same word that is used to describe Christ's transfiguration on the mountain is also applied to each one of us who has opened our hearts to him in faith and obedience.

Some time ago a striking looking man walked into my office. He was tall and blond and tanned. He fairly glittered. He had success written all over his appearance. So when he said he was from Beverly Hills, I really wasn't surprised. But as handsome as he was, and as successful as he appeared, this man was in great need. His marriage had blown up. He was in serious debt. On the surface he was great, but beneath the surface there was pain, there was failure, there was the realization that he needed God. We met several times, and eventually he committed his life to Christ and began to grow. But then his job took him away to another city, a place where I feared that the world, the flesh, and the devil—one or the other, or all three—would simply overwhelm him again. I didn't see him for some time. Not long ago, we met again, and I was bowled over at the change in this man—the change for the better! Instead of backsliding, he had matured. His words, his aims, his motives, his manner, his relationships, all are now more Christlike than I could have dreamed, particularly considering where he has been living. The Hollywood glitter is gone, but it has been replaced by a different sort of light— the light of Christ. You can see it when he talks. You can see it when he smiles. He is in the process of transfiguration, you see. He is experiencing his own transfiguration.

To understand this, let's think back to an event in the Old Testament, found in the book of Exodus. Moses had been receiving the law of God on the holy mountain:

> When Moses came down from Mount Sinai, with the two tablets of the testimony in his hand, Moses did not know that the skin of his face shone because he had been talking with God. And when Aaron and all the people of Israel saw Moses, behold, the skin of his face shone, and they were afraid to come near him.... And when Moses had finished speaking with them, he put a veil over his face; but whenever Moses went in before the Lord to speak with him, he took the veil off, until he came out; and when he came out and told the people of Israel what he was commanded, the people of Israel saw the face of Moses, that the skin of Moses' face shone; and Moses would put the veil upon his face again, until he went in to speak with him. (Exod. 34:29-30,33-35)

St. Paul, many years later, picked this story up:

> Now if the dispensation of death, carved in letters on stone [the old covenant], came with such splendor that the Israelites could not look at

Moses' face because of its brightness, fading as it was, will not the dispensation of the Spirit [the new covenant] be attended with greater splendor....Since we.... are very bold, not like Moses who put a veil over his face so that the Israelites might not see the end of the fading splendor....And we all, with unveiled face, beholding the glory of the Lord, are being changed into his likeness from one degree of glory to another; for this comes from the Lord who is the Spirit. (2 Cor. 3:7-8, 12-13, 18)

Here is Moses, with the radiant glory of the Lord reflecting from his face. Whenever he met with God his appearance was transfigured. He removed his veil in the presence of God. Eventually the light would fade, but Moses would cover his face, because he did not want people to see that God's reflection was fading. He was still struggling, probably wanting to be a little more and a little better than he was. We all struggle to be completely honest about where we really are. "Now," says St. Paul, "if Moses reflected God's presence, Moses who only had the Old Testament law and not the Good News of Christ, and was filled only momentarily with the Holy Spirit, how much more can we who are indwelt by the Holy Spirit reflect it?"

So, when the Holy Spirit comes into our life, he begins the work of transformation. He changes us gradually, and he works within us to help us become more and more like Christ. And that is *our* transfiguration. It's just as real as what happened to Jesus. The process has already begun. We are being changed on the inside. And at the last day, when Christ takes us to heaven, the process will be completed. Paul describes this:

Just as we have borne the image of the man of dust [just as we have been flesh and blood], we shall also bear the image of the man of heaven [in other words, we are becoming like Christ]...Lo! I tell you a mystery. We shall not all sleep, but we shall

all be changed, in a moment, in the twinkling of an eye, at the last trumpet. For the trumpet will sound, and the dead will be raised imperishable, and we shall be changed. For this perishable nature must put on the imperishable, and this mortal nature must put on immortality. (1 Cor. 15:49,51-53)

In other words, when Christ comes into our life he begins to change us, and when he comes for us at the end and takes us to the next life, the change is completed—and we are like Christ as much as a person can be. Charles Wesley wrote a hymn about this entitled "Love Divine, All Loves Excelling." In this hymn, he prays:

Finish then thy new creation, pure and spotless let us be,
Changed from glory into glory, till in heaven we take our place,
Till we cast our crowns before thee, lost in wonder, love, and praise.

We are in the process right now of being changed. And it will be consummated at the end. Now, how does this transfiguration take place? Does it just happen automatically, no matter what you do—without effort? No. Hardly. In his letter to the Christians at Rome St. Paul picks up this same theme again:

Do not be conformed to this world but be transformed [or transfigured. How?] by the renewal of your mind (Rom.12:2).

What does that mean? First, transformation is a command. The process of being transformed is something to which we must commit ourselves firmly. We must want it and give ourselves to it. But, secondly, the command is in the present continual tense. In other words, it is something that goes on for a long time—something that keeps on happening. Each day we must recommit ourselves afresh.

The process is not completed short of heaven. But note that the last point—"be transformed"—is in the passive tense. In other words, we do not transform ourselves, but rather we must let the Holy Spirit do it within us. The Holy Spirit was not given to us primarily for enjoyment, but was given to us to work wonderful changes in us. How? St. Paul says, "by the renewing of your mind." What does that mean? It means by learning to think like Christ. As we learn to think like Christ, we look at life more and more from God's perspective. Christ helps us. And our decisions about what is good or bad are based more and more consistently on God's word and Christ's example. And as we learn to think like Christ, then we begin to act like Christ, and as we begin to act like Christ, we become transformed—we become more and more like Christ. We do it in cooperation with the Holy Spirit. It is impossible truly to do this apart from the indwelling of the Holy Spirit and the encouragement of other believers.

Every person who has put his or her faith in Christ is in the process of transfiguration. If you have been a Christian for eighty-five years, you are still being changed. If you have been a believer for five hours, you are being changed. Everybody who has put their faith in Christ is in the process of transformation. The person in the pew next to you is an eternal, immortal being. If that person loves Christ—however imperfectly—he or she will live for ever and ever in the timeless glory of heaven. And right now, the power of God is at work in that person, bringing about transformation. You can see it in the faces of some people. You can hear it in the words of some people. You can sense it in the actions of some people. But, even if you cannot see it, it is still happening. Don't judge the person by what you can or cannot see right now. That person is in process. But if we could have the physical aspect stripped away, as happened before the disciples on that holy mountain, and actually see the glory of God at work inside that person, it would be something like what the disciples saw at Jesus' transfiguration. The glory of God is at work in the lives of those who believe. And one day we will see it with our eyes. For now, we catch some glimpses. For the most part we trust it, we accept it by faith.

Once a man brought home a tree, and he planted it in his back yard. It was fall, and nothing marked out this tree as particularly unusual, but when spring came, the tree grew leaves and tiny pink buds that became beautiful pink blossoms. The man thought, "How wonderful! A flowering tree. I'll enjoy its beauty all summer." But then, before he had time to enjoy the flowers, the wind began to blow, and all the petals were on the ground in the yard. "What a mess," he thought, "this tree isn't any good after all." Summer passed. One day, the man noticed that the tree was full of little green fruit, the size of nuts. He found a large one and took a bite—"Uh! Bitter." He threw it on the ground. "What a horrible taste," he said. "This tree is worthless. The flowers are so fragile, the wind blows them away. Its fruit is terrible and bitter. When winter comes, I'm going to cut this tree down." But the tree paid no attention to the man and continued to draw water from the ground and light from the sun, and late in the fall, it produced a big crop of bright, crisp, red apples.

Here is an analogy of the Christian life. Sometimes we see Christians who are new in their faith. They have the early blossoms of joy and happiness, and we think they should stay that way forever. Or we see bitterness in the life of a Christian, and we are sure that they will never become joyful or transformed. Could it be that we are forgetting that we are all in the process of being changed? Don't be discouraged. Don't give up. The glorious presence of God is at work, and you and I are being changed. As we look to God, as we cling to God, as we meditate on God's word, as we fail and then repent, God is at work. We are not yet what we are going to be, but thank God, we are not what we used to be.

Any maturing Christian will undergo enormous changes in outlook over the years. You can think probably of some major changes that have taken place in your life regarding your attitude towards certain people, your personal life goals, the way you now approach certain situations, etc. Perhaps your children or your mate or a close friend could greatly benefit from your telling how you have changed and why.

For further meditation: Philippians 1:3-11

Reflective Questions to Ask Myself

1. Jesus often went away to be alone for a while before making a major decision or prior to important steps in his life—do I do this? Do I need more solitude in my life? Do I need to be still before God and listen more? How can I do this?

2. Am I more of a Christlike person than I was when I was half the age I am now? What are two or three ways I have matured? Take a few minutes to thank God for this.

3. Am I trying to change something in my life right now that I know is wrong? Have I sincerely asked the Holy Spirit to work this change in me?

5

DEATH

"The end of birth is death;
the end of death is birth:
this is ordained."

Sir Edwin Arnold

"Is death the last sleep?
No, it is the last and final awakening."

Sir Walter Scott

It was now about the sixth hour, and there was darkness over the whole land until the ninth hour, while the sun's light failed; and the curtain of the temple was torn in two. Then Jesus, crying with a loud voice, said, "Father, into thy hands I commit my spirit!" And having said this he breathed his last. *(Luke 23:44-46)*

None of us knows when or how we will die, but we do all know with certainty that unless Christ returns soon, we, too, will die. These bodies of ours will give out and give up. Dying is inevitable. This week, I put three of my children on the airplane to go visit family and relatives, and when I did, I thought, "I may never see them again." Every time you pull out into traffic on a busy road you do it at risk of your life. Whenever you slip on your jogging shoes, or even go for a walk around the block, you know it could be for the last time. We don't dwell on it, we hardly ever even think of it that way, but we hear enough stories of heart attacks, hit-and-run victims, and all sorts of sudden and unanticipated violence that we are constantly reminded that death can come at any time. I have been at enough funerals to teach me not to take health and life for granted. And since this year is the first of eleven years during which I will be seeking to put five children through college, I recently committed myself to a sizeable increase in my life insurance policy—just in case!

On the church calendar, Passion Sunday begins the most holy week of the year. It is the one specific time in the Christian calendar when we are forced to be reminded clearly and specially of the death of Christ and our own death. Can a person be ready for death? Can we really ever prepare? Yes. How? By understanding the death of Christ and by knowing what it means to be crucified with Christ.

First, let us consider the death of Christ. Long before Good Friday, Jesus had committed himself to the cross, because it was absolutely essential to God's plan. Someone has said, "The cross is the crux of the Bible. The Old Testament looks forward to the cross, the New Testament looks back to the cross." "The Son of man," said Jesus, speaking about himself, "must suffer and be slain." He came, he said, to give up his life. Jesus shared with his disciples that he must go to Jerusalem and suffer many things and be killed (Matt. 16:21). St. John tells us that Jesus said about his life, "No one takes it from me. I lay it down, myself" (John 10:18).

As he gradually realized that it was his Father's will that he die young, Jesus accepted it, and therefore, when the time came, he was ready. He was prepared to die. This does not mean it was easy for him. In fact, there have been few deaths as hard or as horrible as Christ's. First, he was flogged without mercy by two burly Roman soldiers, who used whips of leather thongs of various lengths with small iron balls or bits of broken sheep bones tied at intervals. That was intended to weaken a person just short of collapse—or just short of death. Then, with his back sliced to the bone, he was forced to carry on his bloody back his own hard cross. After that, he had rough iron spikes between five and seven inches long with square shafts driven through his wrists and his feet to attach him to the hard wood of the cross, which caused excruciating pain and paralysis. But it was probably the fact that it was almost impossible to breathe while hanging on a cross that finally killed him. He suffocated, after hanging naked for several hours before a crowd. Cicero, the Roman statesman, called it the most cruel, most hideous form of death.

But other people have died horrible deaths. What made Jesus' death so awful? It was not just the manner, but the fact that he took upon himself punishment for all the sins of humankind. The punishment that God's justice demands, had to be carried out for every single wrong that has ever been done. He felt the full force, the pain, the agony, the loneliness of every whipping, every beating, every jail sentence, every lonely year in prison, the agony of every hangman's noose, the jolt of every electric chair's killing voltage. All of that, Jesus took upon himself. It was so painful that even the sun in the sky hid its face for three hours. Darkness covered the face of the earth, so that it was hidden from everyone, and no one knew the extent of suffering that our Lord endured.

A Scotsman's Death

When I was a young man, I spent several years in the university town of Princeton, New Jersey. The chaplain of the university, Ernest Gordon, became a friend of mine. A Scotsman, he had been a chaplain during World War II and used to tell us of his experiences during the war. Of special interest to us were the stories he told of his difficult days as a prisoner in a Japanese prisoner of war camp. One story that particularly impressed me was of another Scotsman who was also a prisoner.

The soldiers had been impressed by their captors for a work detail on the railroad. As one day's work was ending, the tools were being counted. The Japanese guard declared that one of the shovels was missing and insisted that one of the prisoners had stolen it and sold it to the Thais. The man became livid with anger as he demanded to know who had stolen the tool. Finally, he shouted with uncontrollable fury that all would die unless the thief came forward! As he raised his rifle to take aim, no one doubted that he would commence firing.

At that moment, Gordon told us, a Scotsman stepped forward, stood at attention, and said, "I did it." Immediately the guard loosed all his fury on this man, bringing the rifle butt crashing down upon the prisoner's head, kicking him and beating him with his fists. The soldier sank to the ground and did not move. It was quite clear to everyone that he was dead, his skull smashed by the blow of the rifle butt, but the guard continued to beat his lifeless body until he finally stopped, exhausted.

The other men of the work detail grimly lifted their comrade's body and carried him back to the camp. Later, the tools were counted again at the guard house, and it was found that no shovel was missing after all.

This man who did not deserve to die himself still willingly took upon himself the pain of a horrible death, so that his brethren might be saved. So, too, did Jesus give himself willingly for us.

How could he go willingly to a death like that? How could he resist when that jeering voice from the crowd called out, "If you are the Son of God, come down from the cross?" He could have stepped down if he had so chosen. But three years before, alone in the desert, he had settled once and for all—that he would not use spectacular miracles to establish his Kingdom. He could have come down from the cross had he so willed it, but his love for you and for me bound him more tightly to the cross than the nails and ropes which held his body. We can only guess that it was the assurance that he had in advance that he would come through it and rise from the dead that enabled him to go to the cross. He was not the only one who suffered. How the Father in heaven must have suffered as his Son faced this horrible death—so necessary, so wonderful in what it brought about, but so awful.

I shall never forget how anguished and grief-stricken my wife and I were when some years ago, our own son had a terrible fall, head first onto cement. In anguish and excruciating pain, eventually out of his mind, he thrashed about and cried as they tied him down until he couldn't move, and then they lowered him into that frightening tunnel where they do brain scans, so that they could examine the fractures in his skull and the bleeding underneath. We knew it had to be done, and we were grateful that it *could* be done, but our little boy's pain was almost more than we could take.

The precious gift of forgiveness for our sins cost the Father just as it cost the Son, but the price they paid has purchased for us a promise which enables us now to look at our coming death from a totally new perspective: the perspective of the resurrection.

Let us consider our own death. How are we to look at our death? Is it a period? Is it the end? Or is it, as someone has said, a conjunction, simply a connection with something else? Well, the person who has no belief in the supernatural would say it's simply the end, and when you die you die. You *are* no longer. The candle is snuffed out. It's over. The *New Ager* says that dying is simply part of an ongoing process, and that we can look forward to another life here on earth—later on, the next time around.

We do not see death that way, because of Christ and his death and resurrection. The one who puts his trust in Christ sees death differently. We see death, in a sense, like a tunnel—a tunnel under a roadway, where you can, by kneeling, look through and see light on the other side. And even as we enter that tunnel, we know that we will soon emerge in the light of a new day. We are not exactly certain of what it is like in the tunnel, but we are only there for a few moments. Then we find ourselves in a heavenly world, where there is no more night, no more wrong, and no more suffering. I sometimes think the most beautiful words that Jesus ever spoke were just before his death, when he was talking to the disciples about death:

> Let not your hearts be troubled; believe in God, believe also in me. In my Father's house are many mansions; if it were not so, would I have told you that I go to prepare a place for you? And...I will come again to receive you. (John 14:1-3)

Wonderful words of promise. And for those who have given themselves to Christ, these words take great meaning. We cling to them.

Two Kinds of Death

There are two kinds of death that we must go through. The last death is when the body dies. That is the end of life here in this world. But there is an earlier death which is not a physical death. It is more a spiritual sort of death, and it happens when we turn away from the way of self and give as much of ourselves as we can to as much of Christ as we know. Dietrich Bonhoeffer, a German Lutheran hero of the 1940s, said that when Christ calls a person he calls that person to come and die. Now you might say, "But I thought Christ called us to come and live the abundant life." Yes, he calls us to live, but we learn to live by dying first. St. Paul called it our "own crucifixion":

> I have been crucified with Christ and I myself alone no longer live, but Christ lives in me; and the real life I now have within this body is the result of my trusting in the Son of God, who loved me and gave himself for me. (Gal.2:20)

The old me has died. That was Volume One. And now Christ is in us and we have begun Volume Two. And if you have accepted this Good News, then God's life lives in you. And, in a sense, a part of you is in heaven already. Now, as this happens, we have seen that we begin to change—our perspective, our values, our priorities, and our dreams begin to become more those of God. And every time you catch yourself giving in to temper, or jealousy, or this or that addiction, or to a pattern of thinking characteristic of the old, wrong way, you stop and say, "That's the old me! He's been crucified. I don't have to live that way anymore."

I know a man who, when his wife became angry with him, criticized him, or jumped on him, would invariably become angry back. He would become defensive and would wallow in self-pity, and would think of retorts to make. One day, he realized how foolish, selfish and wrong it was. He realized that he did not have to react that way, and he began to ask God to make his new nature strong in times like that. Sometimes he still fails, but he is infinitely better now. And the interesting thing is that as that part of him has been crucified, he is less afraid of dying. A crucified person has nothing to fear in death.

Let us try to stretch our imaginations to understand this more clearly. Imagine that there was a man who had two fruit trees in his garden. He lived in a magical world where an orange tree and an apple tree would both grow at the same time in the same place. He loved those oranges, but whenever he ate one he became sick. Finally, he was found to be allergic to the citrus of the orange fruit. So he took his ax and cut the root of the orange tree, and he killed it. But for a long while those beautiful oranges still hung on the tree. He came to love apples, but once in a while, the oranges looked so good that he would go back and eat an orange, only to become sick again. You see, the root had been severed, but the fruit was still there. The same is true with us and the cross. In the cross, the root of our sin has been severed, but the fruit—the old habits, the old ways of thinking—is still there. What that man should have done is to take those oranges one by one and throw them over the backyard fence. We need to learn to toss those old ways out, one by one, and to enjoy and thrive on the fruit of the Holy Spirit—it takes time. All of this is a part of our first death. And every time you toss another orange over the fence, more and more of yourself is ready for that second death, when your body will die, because you have given more of the territory of your life to God, and you are more ready for the new life. God alone knows when he is ready to take you to heaven and when you are fit to be taken. The more we know of Christ, the more prepared we are for the next life. The more we know of him, the more territory we want to yield to him. And the time comes, eventually, when we are ready to die.

I watched a good and wonderful man go through this process years ago. As he grew older, he gave more and more of his life to the Lord. He had been a believer all of his life, and a churchman, but I watched him give his business and those concerns to God. God came first. I watched him give his habits to the Lord. I watched him give his family. I even watched him give his reputation to God. Christ loomed larger and larger in his life as he moved through his sixties. Then he fell ill, and in his illness he told me that he had had a vision of Christ standing beside his bed in the hospital. And the wonder of Christ, as he saw him, was more wonderful than he could describe. But as he told me about it in the intensive care room of the hospital, his face lit up. He said, "Son, when I looked at him, I knew that if he wanted me, I was ready." My dad had never said that before, but as Christ became larger in his vision he became ready. And within forty-eight hours of his having said that to me, he went into the next life.

Dying is inevitable, but dying in peace is a choice. If you really want to be prepared to die in peace, then learn how to live now in the way God is calling you to live. Turn away from the old ways which have been nailed to the cross with Christ. Look to him and let him loom larger and larger with each day. Then when he comes for you, you'll be ready, too.

Have you made the effort to talk with those who are closest to you about the eventuality of your own death? Do they know how you feel about dying? Do they know what you would like to be remembered for and what your desires are for your own funeral?

For further meditation: 1 Corinthians 15

Reflective Questions to Ask Myself

1. Is it important to me that when I have died those who are influenced by my life will think of me with gratitude and fondness?

2. What things would I like those at my funeral to remember about me?

3. Am I clear enough in my words and habits now so that when I am dead there will be no question about my devotion to Jesus Christ?

4. "Lord Jesus Christ, open my eyes and mind to see these areas of my own life that you still desire to put to death, that my motives and ideals might be more yours and less mine."

6

RESURRECTION

"Immortal Hope dispels the gloom!
An angel sits beside the tomb."

Sarah Flower Adams

But the angel said to the women, "Do not be afraid;
for I know that you seek Jesus who was crucified. He
is not here; for he has risen, as he said. Come, see the
place where he lay. Then go quickly and tell his disciples that he has risen from the dead, and behold, he is
going before you to Galilee; there you will see him.
Lo, I have told you so." *(Matt. 28:5-7)*

One of my favorite places in the world is North
Carolina. Down amongst those sunbleached sand dunes in
Kitty Hawk, there is one huge grass-covered hill with a
massive concrete monument at its crest. It was placed
there years ago in honor of an idea that seemed utter foolishness to most people. To two bachelor brothers from
Ohio, however, it was an obsession and an utter certainty
which they pursued over and over again, convinced that
this was an idea whose time had come. Wilbur Wright
wrote a letter to a friend on May 13, 1900: "For some
years," he said, "I have been afflicted with the belief that
flight is possible to man. My disease has increased in
severity and I feel that it will soon cost me an increased
amount of money, if not my life. I have been trying to
arrange my affairs in such a way that I can devote my entire time, for a few months, to experiments in this field."[2]

It turned out, of course, that this dream of flying was
not foolishness, and the Wright brothers' successful self-
propelled flight three years later proved it. It could be ar-

gued that no other technological development of the last century has made a greater impact on humankind than the achievement of flight. It has been absolutely central to our view and experience of modern civilization. All over the planet, life is different. It will never be the same again. As long ago as 1961, astronauts were travelling around the world at a speed of 16,000 miles an hour. They say that sometime in the next century we will just hop on a shuttle and be in Tokyo in half an hour—all because a handful of people adamantly believed in an idea that most people thought was ridiculous.

Christians gather to worship every week because of *another* radical idea, a concept that at first seemed absolutely ridiculous and even today still seems utter foolishness to millions of people. It makes no practical sense; it certainly cannot be scientifically verified; but those who believe it are absolutely convinced of its certainty and cannot imagine a world in which one could live successfully without this truth. And I am speaking, of course, about the resurrection—the resurrection and its power in our lives.

If I were to ask you what word most sums up the Christian life, what would you say? It is *resurrection*. This is the most characteristic word of our faith. More than any other, this is the theme that we rally around, Sunday after Sunday. This is the hope that God offers a world that is so often dashed in confusion and chaos.

Sometimes we tend to think of God's Son hanging on the cross as the ultimate, most moving symbol of our faith. But as important as Good Friday is, it is not the end, and it is not the final image of Christianity. The final image, is an empty cross, trampled in the dirt by a risen Lord Jesus Christ. Were it not for the resurrection and all that's happened as a result of those who have trusted in it, there would be no church, there would be no New Testament. In fact, without the resurrection, life on earth itself would be dramatically, shockingly different, unbelievably impoverished.

What does the resurrection mean? Well, if Jesus had been evil, then his rising from the dead would be the most frightening of all events, because it would indicate that evil ultimately triumphs over good, and that, finally, the meanest, the most selfishly aggressive, the least scrupulous will win. Indeed, life does sometimes seem to be that way. But because Jesus is *good*, and his character, and the record of his actions, words, and teachings always reflect an unshakable commitment to mercy, kindness, self-sacrifice and love, his resurrection gives us hope that ultimately *good* will prevail over *evil* and that right is stronger than might. What a wonderful truth!

But that is just the beginning of what resurrection means. It also means that Jesus was filled with the presence of God. The resurrection convinces us that what he taught is indeed true—not only his moral teachings, but also his claim to a unique relationship with the Father, and his teaching that in his death, a cosmic transaction occurred in which the sins of humankind were punished. The one human being who never sinned took upon himself God's necessary and just punishment so that all of us might receive forgiveness.

Jesus' resurrection means that and still more. It means that Jesus is alive. He is *alive*. Do you really *have* that thought? Does that thought really have you? Think about it! It means that he is as alive as we are—living, acting, interacting. It is the most spectacular truth I can imagine. This radiant, compassionate, living Master is walking beside *us*, in *our* sorrows and troubles, just as he walked on the road to Emmaus with those two depressed disciples on the first Easter day.

His resurrection means even more. It means that he is Lord, that we are to keep his commandments, and that in the way that he laid down for us, we can find *our way* most successfully as well.

The resurrection means that there is power in Jesus, a power greater than death. The New Testament writers called it *dunamis*—dynamite power. It is the same power that gave sight to blind eyes, that straightened out and strengthened withered arms and paralyzed legs; it is the same power that commanded a frightening storm on the Sea of Galilee to "hush and be still"; the same power that pushed up the Rockies and carved out the depths of the ocean. The power of almighty God himself is seen to be at work in the resurrection of Jesus.

All of these things are implied in the resurrection—the triumph of good over evil, the divinity of Christ, his Lordship, the validation of his words and his teachings, the fact that his way is *the* way, the unique significance of his death for us, and the power of God at work in our lives.

But there is even more to the resurrection than this. The resurrection is not just something out there. It is not just a single shining event on the horizon of history. The resurrection has something to do with you and me right now. I am told that in the Battle of Waterloo, there was one spot on the battlefield that was so crucial, it was taken and retaken by Napoleon, and then by Wellington, three times—so essential was that piece of ground to winning the victory. And I am told that it was one of the keys to the ultimate victory of the British. The resurrection is like that for us. It wasn't just crucial for Jesus and for the early church—it is also crucial for each one of us. The resurrection is essential if we are going to experience the Christian life today. For just as Jesus experienced the resurrection, you, too can experience the resurrection. You can, and I can.

St. Paul spoke of this very thing:

If then you have been raised with Christ, seek the things that are above, where Christ is, seated at the right hand of God. Set your mind on things that are above, not on things that are on earth. For you have died, and your life is hid with Christ in God. When Christ who is our life appears, then you also will appear with him in glory. (Col. 3:1-4)

Now what is that all about? Is he just talking about the end of time, when Christ said he would actually return in his heavenly splendor to destroy all evil forever and set up his eternal kingdom? The Bible calls that the final resurrection, the last day, when all who love him will be clothed with an eternal, resurrected body forever. No, that event is something beyond us still. It is yet to be, and too deep for us at present even to understand. No, St. Paul is describing a resurrection that is in the past tense. He said, "You *have been* raised up with Christ." Could it be that there is some way whereby we, today, can share in the resurrection power of Christ? Yes. That is really what it's about. The very same energy that raised Christ up from the grave, after he had been dead for three days, is available for you, for me, and for any who would receive it. And that has to be the final explanation for that uncontainable excitement and enthusiasm of the first-century Christians.

The Scottish theologian James Stewart said this:

Never did an enterprise look more utterly ruined than when Jesus of Nazareth was taken down from the cross and laid in the tomb. He was crucified, dead and buried, says our Apostles' Creed. And the very words seem burdened with an awful finality. If the disciples thought about the future at all, they saw themselves creeping back, shamefacedly to the homes they had once left so eagerly at Jesus' bidding. And they hurt in their minds in fancying the jeers and taunts of the village street as they so ingloriously returned.[3]

These men and women, the early Christians, were just like us. They had nothing unusual about them. They had their own personal host of problems. Morally and spiritually they had failed many times. But then on the first Easter evening, the risen Jesus appeared to them, and they said, "God has brought him back from the dead! And he has said that we too may share in this power!" And this lit-

tle band of men and women cowering in an upper room
were so filled with the resurrection power of God that they
went forth, without education, without plans, without
magnetic personalities, without financial backing, without
government support. They didn't even have any private
foundation grants. And they turned the world upside
down, simply because they had been linked with that same
resurrection power. And it has been happening ever since.
All through history, men and women, boys and girls,
whose lives have been touched by the risen Jesus and who
have gotten in touch with resurrection power in their own
lives, have begun to live life on a higher plane.

By "setting their minds on things above," as St. Paul
urged the Colossians, or committing themselves to God's
priorities above all, these people have found God's power
in the midst of their own personal weaknesses. They have
found God's *ability* at work through their own *avail*ability.
They have found God's purposes to be greater than their
own. They found purpose, like a man named Paul
Lawrence Dunbar. Paul Dunbar is the man for whom the
famous Dunbar High School in Washington, D.C. was
named. He was a great black American poet of times gone
by. Dunbar once wrote:

> *The Lord had a job for me but I had so much to do*
> *I said, "You get somebody else or wait 'til I get through."*
> *I don't know how the Lord came out, but he seemed to get*
>   *along,*
> *But I felt kind of sneaking like, knowed I done God wrong.*
> *One day I needed the Lord, needed him right away,*
> *But he never answered me at all. I could hear him say,*
> *Down in my accusing heart, "Brother, I'se got too much to*
>   *do,*
> *You get somebody else or wait'll I get through."*
> *Now, when the Lord he have a job for me I never try to shirk,*
> *I drops whatever I have on hand and does the good Lord's*
>   *work,*
> *And my affairs can run along or wait 'til I get through,*
> *Nobody else can do the work God has marked out for you.*

God's purpose is done through the power of God. Do we really realize the resurrected life that God has for us?

Samuel Johnson said about the novelist Oliver Goldsmith, "He would be a great man if he realized the wealth of his internal resources." I wonder whether you have begun to realize the wealth of your internal resources through the power of the risen Christ.

I know that we hear preachers give such challenges today, and sometimes we say, "Well, really I don't think God could do much through me. We can't really live today the sort of life that Christ and the early Christians lived. The complexities of modern life are just too great. I've tried prayer, I've even read the Bible some, but it just doesn't seem to work that way." But let me say something very gently and kindly: the problem is not a lack of resurrection power; the problem is that we stopped trying a long time ago. We didn't really expect to be able to live that way. But St. Paul and those first-century men and women would look at us today, and they would shout out, "Do you really think your problems and the complexities that you are grappling with are going to bewilder God and overwhelm that power that raised Jesus from the dead? Can't the God that brought Jesus back from the dead, if you ask him, release his own power as well in you and me?"

There is one condition, and it is noted in that little word *if* at the beginning of those four verses that Paul wrote. "If," he said, "you have been raised with Christ..." then. And the meaning of that condition is found two lines later, in three words: "you have died." *If* you have died you can be raised with Christ. What does that mean? We have already discussed it in the last chapter. The condition is this: before the power of God can be fully experienced in our life, before we can know the peace of God, before we can have hope in eternal life beyond the grave, one thing is needed—we must surrender ourselves to Christ. That is what Paul means by *dying*.

Before the resurrected life can be real in my life, I first

have to set aside my prideful ways, my wants, my own selfish plans, so that *my history* is changed into *his story* in *my* life. Many sincere church-going people, including many clergy of all denominations, are still committed first to their own plans, and only secondly to God's concerns. But scripture tells us, "If you would be raised with Christ, then first you must die to what is not of Christ." The road to resurrection leads first by the cross. And only you know what that means in your life. But once the cross becomes real in our life, then the power of the resurrection begins to permeate our life, which before was without power, without eternal purpose, just as a limp dangling glove, becomes filled with strength, power, and purpose when you place your hand in it.

Years ago, grateful citizens raised a monument to the Wright brothers for their unshakable commitment to an idea that they knew to be real. They pursued it until they realized it. Now, what sort of monument will they raise to us Christians at the end of the twentieth century? I hope, I trust, and I pray that it will be a monument that says about us: "They were people of the resurrection." People of the resurrection.

✠ ✠ ✠ ✠ ✠ ✠ ✠ ✠ ✠ ✠

You will not know if the resurrection power of Christ is powerfully at work within you unless you commit yourself to things that simply on your own you are unable to achieve. It may be something within your own life, or it may be a huge task desperately in need of doing, but beyond your personal ability. If you only tackle those things that you know you can achieve on your own, you may miss out on the miraculous resurrection power of Christ working through you.

For further meditation: Matthew 17:14-20

Reflective Questions to Ask Myself

1. Have I seen Christ's resurrection power at work in some way in my own life? in another's life? Have I given him credit?

2. Do I tend to focus more on my own ability, or on being faithfully available to the Lord and trusting in his abilities, as I encounter needs in the world? My ability or his ability?

3. Have I missed vital opportunities because I trusted his power too little?

4. Is there some situation now before me that I will begin to pray about in which Christ's resurrection power can be realized through me, or through others, as we step forward in faith?

7

ASCENSION

Thou hast raised our human nature
On the clouds to God's right hand:
There we sit in heav'nly places,
There with thee in glory stand.
Jesus reigns, adored by angels;
Man with God is on the throne;
Mighty Lord, in thine ascension,
We by faith behold our own.

Christopher Wordsworth

So when they had come together, they asked him, "Lord, will you at this time restore the kingdom to Israel?" He said to them, "It is not for you to know times or seasons which the Father has fixed by his own authority. But you shall receive power when the Holy Spirit has come upon you; and you shall be my witnesses in Jerusalem and in all Judea and Samaria and to the end of the earth." And when he had said this, as they were looking on, he was lifted up, and a cloud took him out of their signt. And while they were gazing into heaven as he went, behold, two men stood by them in white robes, and said, "Men of Galilee, why do you stand looking into heaven? This Jesus, who was taken up from you into heaven, will come in the same way as you saw him go into heaven." (*Acts 1:6-11*)

A few years ago, our family was in Switzerland for a couple of weeks, and we set out one day in the car to climb up into the Alps. Every turn seemed to take us to a lovelier view. First there were lovely vistas of green pastures and streams. Then higher up there were hills and waterfalls, then higher still there were gorgeous meadows of wild flowers, with cows feeding and bells around their necks tinkling in a melodious way. Finally, we came out on the top, and all around us towered awesome and majestic snow-covered peaks. They seemed to be reaching out their arms to call us. Now the life of Christ is like that in some ways. First you look at the story of his birth, then at his baptism, then at his temptation, his teaching, his miracles, then Good Friday, then Easter—and every step in his life seems to be more wonderful than the last. You feel that there is so much there, so much power, beauty, and mystery, that you can't take it all in.

At the top of those mountains, we came to a quaint little guest house for travellers which we entered for a rest and a meal. As we entered, we were overwhelmed and almost breathless over the beauty that was around us, but we found that the folks working there in that little inn were almost oblivious to—in some ways, even apparently bored with—the beauty that was all around them, because it was nothing new to them. They were familiar with it; they took it for granted. When we look at the life of Christ, and when we come to this last, momentous time in his life on earth, we should beware of being like the Swiss innkeeper, becoming blasé, just taking it all for granted. After all, we have heard a thousand times the words, "He ascended into heaven. He is seated at the right hand of the Father." But in some ways, this is the loveliest and most triumphant of all the moments in Christ's life, and it is certainly one of the most unusual. You don't have a complete picture of Christ's life unless you understand the ascension. Let us look at the ascension from three perspectives: one, what happened; two, what it meant for him; and, finally, what it means for us.

First of all, *what happened?* The first chapter of Acts gives the fullest picture of this story. After the resurrection says St. Luke:

He presented himself to the disciples alive after his

passion by many proofs, appearing to them during forty days, and speaking of the kingdom of God. And while staying with them he charged them not to depart from Jerusalem, but to wait for the promise of the Father, which, he said, "you heard from me, for John baptized with water, but before many days you shall be baptized with the Holy Spirit."

So when they had come together, they asked him... "Lord, will you at this time restore the kingdom to Israel?" He said to them, "It is not for you to know times or seasons which the Father has fixed by his own authority. But you shall receive power when the Holy Spirit has come upon you; and you shall be my witnesses in Jerusalem and in all Judea and Samaria and to the end of the earth." And when he had said this, as they were looking on, he was lifted up, and a cloud took him out of their sight. And while they were gazing into heaven as he went, behold, two men stood by them in white robes, and said, "Men of Galilee, why do you stand looking up into heaven? This Jesus, who was taken up from you into heaven, will come in the same way as you saw him go into heaven." (Acts 1:3-11)

During the time from the resurrection up until this moment in the story, the Lord had withdrawn from his disciples several times. Every time he withdrew, he returned. Where did he go during those times?

On Easter morning, right after the resurrection, Jesus told Mary Magdalene that he was on his way to the Father. We think that after the resurrection he returned quietly and secretly to the presence of the Father. Then he returned. Later he withdrew again, and again, but each time he would return to reassure the disciples that he was alive, to encourage them, to teach and instruct them further and to prepare them for his final withdrawal. It is not that he went *away* from them so much as he occasionally withdrew from their presence into the full presence of God the Father during these forty days.

But then, on the last day, he gathered his followers together just outside the walls of the old city, on the Mount of Olives. He commanded them not to leave Jerusalem until they received the Holy Spirit which he would send. He told them it was his will that they become his witnesses all over the world. Then, simply and soberly, Luke describes what happened: "He was lifted into the sky into a luminous cloud and disappeared."

St. John Chrysostom, preaching in the fourth century, said, "The royal chariot was sent for Jesus and he was taken." And everyone there saw it. His public, earthly career was over.

Now, for those who only believe in what they can see, this is hard to believe, but for the one who believes in the supernatural power of God, the ascension should not be any more difficult to believe in than the resurrection. And the way the story is told leads me to believe that had a hard-bitten, twentieth-century Washington journalist been there that day on the hillside, he or she, too, would have seen this event just as the disciples described it.

The Gospel of John says that Jesus had told the disciples in advance that this would happen. As far back in scripture as the Psalms, the ascension of Christ was predicted, and in the New Testament, Mark, Luke, John, Peter, Paul, Stephen, and the writer of Hebrews all talked about the ascension. What actually happened? He simply disappeared. The cloud was a symbol of the holy presence of God—like the cloud that went before the children of Israel through the desert, like the cloud that surrounded Christ and the disciples on the Mount of Transfiguration, revealing the presence of God. And as soon as Jesus was gone, two men dressed in white appeared, who we presume were angels. They announced that he had been taken

into heaven, and one day, in the same way, he would return. That is what happened. He withdrew from their
sight.

Sometimes, this word *heaven* is used in the Bible to describe just the sky above, but here it means more than
that. Usually heaven means that realm where God lives
with all of the angels and all of those who have departed in
faithfulness to him. We talk about going "up" to heaven,
and it appeared as though Jesus were going up. But heaven
is not so much *up* as it is simply *beyond*. Now, here is a
mystery. Heaven is not just above us, but it is very near.
Heaven is there, heaven is here. Heaven is a different realm
of being, of existing. Heaven is the real world. We think
that we live in the real world, and yes, it's *real* enough, but
it is a limited world. Heaven is not limited. It is that realm
where everything is as God desires it to be—perfectly and
permanently. Heaven is as close as we can imagine, yet we
cannot often see it. Heaven existed before our universe. It
exists beside our universe, within it, without it, above it,
beyond it—right here around us. It is that realm where
there are no boundaries, no sense of aging, no sense of
past, no sense of future.

If you have ever read the Narnia tales of C.S. Lewis,
you will understand when I say that heaven is like Narnia.
It is right here, and a person can be taken into heaven just
like that! On a few occasions, people's eyes have been
opened, and they have been able to see into heaven. I believe that from heaven it is possible to see into our limited
universe. Jesus had lived in that realm before he came and
dwelt with us. When he came into our world which is limited by space and time, he saw things from the perspective
of the larger world. And the power of that world was in
him. That is why he said, "The kingdom of heaven has
come upon you." He was able to heal the sick and raise the
dead, although for thirty-three years he subjected himself
to the physical realities of this world. He showed us what
is possible in this physical world if we have our eyes fo-

cused on the larger world in faith. So Jesus, on the day of ascension, withdrew into that larger world. That is what happened.

The second question is: *what did it mean?* What did it mean for him? It meant at least four things. First, the ascension meant that the earthly work of Jesus was brought to a completion. His work on earth was composed of five elements. First, he came to demonstrate that God loved us enough to leave heaven and come and live among us. He accomplished that. Second, he came to communicate and explain God's truth, so that we could understand and know God. He accomplished that. Third, he came to be an example to us as to how to live. He did that. Fourth, he came to reconcile us to God by dying on the cross for our sins. He did that. And, finally, he came to conquer death and open up the pathway to eternal life with the Father. He accomplished that. So the first meaning of the ascension is that he had finished his work and he was going home at last, after a good long day's work.

The second meaning is that his followers, having walked with him and touched and experienced him, were now about to enter into a different relationship with the Lord. In just ten days, they would receive his Holy Spirit into their lives. They were to be empowered with heavenly power. The same is true for us.

The third meaning of his ascension is that just as he departed, one day he will return. And that will be the climax of history. God will then bring the curtain down.

One day, a little girl heard a minister preach about the second coming of Christ and was later quizzing her mother. They were at home, and she said, "Mommy, do you really believe Jesus is going to come back again?" The mother said, "Yes, I do." The girl asked, "Could he come back this week?" "Yes." "Could he come back today?" "Yes." "Could he come in the next hour?" "Yes." "Could he come in a few minutes?" "Yes." (pause.) "Mommy, would you comb my hair, please?" What a wonderful kind of expectancy!

Scripture says he will come back, but there will be some differences. When he left only the Eleven saw him go, but when he comes back, "every eye will see him," (Rev. 1:7). And instead of returning to one particular place, he told the disciples, his return would be "like the lightning which flashes and lights up the sky from one end to another," (Luke 17:23-24).

The Prince Becomes King

At least one other thing was implied in Christ's ascension. In his ascension, we see the return to the Fatherland of the young prince of heaven, now going back to be crowned as the King of kings and Lord of lords. Some time in the next several years, we will probably have a coronation—Prince Charles will become the king of England—and it will be a splendid event. But if you think the coronation of the future king of England will be a mighty event, just imagine the coronation that took place in the Kingdom of God on the Day of Ascension, when Jesus, the King of kings and Lord and lords, was seated on his throne at the right hand of the Father. Writing about this, R.C. Sproul says:

> The ascension of Jesus was the supreme political event in world history. He ascended not so much to a place as to an office...the cosmic King of the universe....The ascension catapulted Jesus to the right hand of God where he was enthroned as King of kings and Lord of lords.[4]

St. Paul described it in this way:

> God raised Christ from death and seated him at his right hand in the heavenly world. Christ rules there above all heavenly rulers, authorities, powers, lords. He has a title superior to all titles of authority in this world and the next. God put all

things under Christ's feet and gave him the church as his body. (Eph. 1:20-25)

We sing about this incredible crowning event, "All hail the power of Jesus' name! Let angels prostrate fall. Bring forth the royal diadem and crown him, crown him, Lord of all!"

Jesus had told even Pilate that this would happen. At Jesus' trial, Pilate had asked, "Are you a king?" And Jesus answered, "Yes, truly, but not of this world"—I am not limited like an earthly ruler, but I am the unlimited king of the universe. This is no spiritual illusion. This is no myth. It is good for us to be reminded that we may deliberate or argue about the ascension, we may honor him, ignore him, disobey him, refuse to serve him or to give ourselves loyally to him, but all the while, he reigns, whatever our response to him is.

All of these things were implied in the ascension. He finished his five-fold work. He began for us a new relationship through the Holy Spirit. As he departed, he announced that he will return one day. And now he rules as king.

But what does the ascension mean for us today? Surely, it couldn't be said that we have an ascension. Wouldn't that be blasphemous? You would think so, and yet, that is exactly what scripture teaches—that in Christ's ascension, we have an ascension too.

In his letter to the church at Ephesus, Paul had been writing about what God did in the life, death, and resurrection of Christ, and what that meant to us, and then he wrote:

God, who is rich in mercy, out of the great love with which he loved us, even when we were dead through our trespasses, made us alive together with Christ [by grace you have been saved], and raised us up with him, and made us sit with him in the heavenly places in Christ Jesus. (Eph.2:4-6)

Past tense! He has already done it. When Christ ascended and sat on the right hand of God, we too were raised; we ascended with him. Earlier, Paul had exclaimed, "Blessed be the God and Father of our Lord Jesus Christ, who has blessed us in Christ with every spiritual blessing in the heavenly places" (Eph. 1:3). Notice he says we are in the heavenly places with Christ.

There is a sense in which it can be said that *we are in heaven with Christ right now.* That is what Paul meant when he wrote to the Philippians, "You are citizens of heaven."

What does it mean when, by faith, you and I opened our lives to Christ? We were indwelt by the Holy Spirit— the real, living life of Christ came to be within us. From that time on we are "in Christ," linked up with him. We are united with him. Where he is, we are, and where we are, he is. And although we are living here on earth, because we are united with him in the Holy Spirit, we too can be said to be living in that other realm, that spiritual realm of heaven, at the right hand of God.

In my Bible I have a snapshot of my wife and me standing by the Dead Sea. I place the photo in an envelope and then place the envelope in the book. Thus the photo of us is in the envelope and in the book at the same time. In a similar way, we here and now live as citizens on the earth. When Christ comes into our lives we are then "*in Christ.*" Christ is in heaven. So we are in the world, but because we are in Christ, we are also in heaven. It is a mystery but powerfully true.

Christ's promise of eternal life is not exactly like a ticket to get into heaven. We are not like a theatergoer who has a prepaid ticket in his pocket, waiting outside the theater to be admitted. No, in our relationship with Christ, we are already in heaven, and when we die, what we now hold onto by faith we will see with our own eyes. Jesus taught, "To know Christ is to have eternal life already."

God, give us eyes to see this. Give us the mind to understand it.

What, then, does this mean for us? Amazing things. When Jesus, God, became a human, he lived among us, and then, in the ascension, he took his humanity back into heaven. Humanity was at the right hand of God, was given power and authority over the evil one. For the first time, humanity had authority over the evil one. This caught the devil by surprise. And now God has given us that authority, because we sit at his right hand, over all evil in the world. And he has given us access to himself. We are as close to God as Christ is. We have the promise of God's attention and God's care, moment by moment. Just as God listens to Christ, he listens to us through Christ, and he hears our prayers. Remember that in the olden days, when someone was to be honored, the person was seated at the right hand of the king, and that meant he had the ear of the king? We are in Christ at the ear of the Father in heaven.

Our ascension also means that because we have ascended spiritually to the presence of God, it makes all the difference in the world in the way we see things here and now and the way we live and think. We see now from God's perspective, not the world's.

Worldliness, a creeping secularism, has seeped into the church and into us. So much of our thinking is materialistic, worldly, and secular, and this is the exact opposite of the goal for which we are to strive. We are to bring the values, the perspectives, and the priorities of heaven, the *real* world, into this world, which is really an unreal world, so that we live and think here and now according to heaven's values. And that means that we learn not to be *beaten* down by the things around us, but to *look* down from our heavenly throne. We have challenges in this earthly life. We have anxieties. We have afflictions. We have addictions. We have dysfunctional families. We have uncertainty in world events. We have unpredictable financial patterns, downturns. There is great uncertainty all around us, and yet these things, as crucial as they are, are just earthly things. And they are small compared to the real world of heaven. There is always a sense in which we can learn to look *down* on these things—what a thought!—from our eternal position of security at the throne of heaven.

This is what Paul was trying to get through to us when he wrote, "Since you have been raised with Christ, keep seeking the things"—the thoughts, the principles, the priorities—"above, where Christ is, seated at the right hand of God" (Col.3:1). Your real life is in heaven, in Christ, with God.

Does that mean we just ignore the things that are going on in our lives? No, we attack them, but with the perspective of heaven. A friend of mine on the West Coast, a retired pastor, Ray Ortlund, described it this way:

> Have you ever seen a bird covered with mud? Obviously if you did the bird would be sick, dying, or dead. It would certainly be unnatural. His sphere is higher; he lives above that kind of contact. Have you seen an earthworm covered with mud? Certainly. Why not?

> So we should never expect natural men without Christ to have spiritual understanding or to display the fruits of the Spirit. They just can't fly.

> But when you see a Christian with mud all over him, with the anxieties and cares and mentality of this world about him, my friend, he's sick. God never intended us to be like that, and we don't need to be.[5]

So, you see, we can keep *looking* down, rather than *being* down. Isn't that what Isaiah meant when he said, "Those who wait on the Lord shall renew their strength, they shall mount up like eagles on wings"?

Let us draw this little book to a close. Sometimes, in reading the Bible, I like to imagine that I am there. Imagine that you were standing on that hillside two thou-

sand years ago with the apostles, listening to Jesus, then
watching. There are two mistakes that some of those people made. Some of those people there were thinking too
much about this world. Remember, they were wondering:
is he going to set up his throne now, is he going to start
ruling, are we going to start making the world all right?
Jesus rebuked them. But then there were others who were
just gazing up at the sky. They were preoccupied with the
spiritual world. John Stott has said that the first vision is
too earthly, but the second is too heavenly. Both were er-
rors that were rebuked.

We can be so caught up in this world that we forget all
about the larger world of heaven. *Or* we can become so
concerned with spiritual things as to be of no earthly use
whatsoever. What the ascension of Jesus calls us to is a
balanced perspective. He gives us a mission here on earth,
and he equips us from heaven. He calls us to live out the
life he lived and to call others to him to work for the bet-
terment of all people, to teach, to heal, to lead, to serve,
and he gives us the means—the person of the Holy
Spirit—and the promise that we are in the process of being
healed, made whole day by day, as we call on his power.
His ascension assures us that because we are united with
him, our home is already in heaven, and that we can rest
in that, even while we are working. We can be sure of our
destiny, even though we feel that, in a sense, we are still
travelling. And even though all around us there is so much
to be done, at the same time, because we have ascended
with Christ to God's right hand, we can look down on all
these things and know that they will be completed. We live
on earth, but we live in heaven, too.

Before you close this book, I invite you to join me in a
little prayer:

We honor you, King of kings, King Jesus—
crowned with all majesty and ruling in all power as
King of kings and Lord of lords. We confess our

smallness before you, our insignificance, and yet we thank you for loving each of us all the way to the cross. Thank you for calling us to yourself, for committing yourself to us, and for allowing us to become joined with you in a mysterious union. Thank you for life here and now on earth, but even more, for eternal life, for drawing us to yourself that we might be with you in heaven even as you are with us here and now.

Teach us, Lord, how to see these things before us now in this earthly life from the perspective of heaven. As we contemplate earthly things help us to be so lifted as to be able to look down to see the end, the resolution as well as what's before us now. And enable us with the power of heaven to accomplish your tasks, our responsibilities here and now, fully, peacefully confident of your presence and your power.

If there have been things in this book that have been helpful to you, perhaps you will want to re-read them, consider them more deeply, and consider how to share what you have learned with others.

For further meditation: 2 Timothy 2:2

Reflective Questions to Ask Myself

1. Have I really allowed God to raise me up to that place where, united with Christ, I am looking down upon my situations from heaven's perspective, or am I mired in the mud of circumstances too much of the time?

2. What practices, experiences, or people have uplifted me in the past so that I have, indeed, been able to have more of Christ's perspective?

3. How might I learn from these recollections to arrange my life henceforth so as to experience more consistently the "ascension perspective"?

NOTES

1. James Boice, *The Gospel of John* (Grand Rapids, Michigan: Zondervan Publishers, 1985), 118.

2. Harry Combs, *Kill Devil Hill* (Englewood, Colorado: TernStyle Press Ltd., 1979), 78.

3. James Stewart, *The Life and Teaching of Jesus Christ* (Nashville: n.d.), 173.

4. R.C. Sproul, *Who Is Jesus?* (Wheaton, Illinois: Tyndale House Publishers, 1983), 94.

5. Ray Ortlund, *Intersections* (Waco, Texas: Word Books, 1979), 149.

LEADER'S GUIDE FOR A GROUP STUDY

INTRODUCTION TO LEADING A SMALL GROUP

One of the best ways to use this book is to pull together a few others, agree to meet regularly, and discuss how these chapters apply to you in your own individual life and in your church life. You do not need to be an experienced leader to lead such a group. After all, the Lord has promised to be with us when we gather in His name, and once people begin to interact with this book and with one another, God has a way of helping us learn from one another and grow in wonderful ways.

The goal of such a group is simply to encourage each other in the challenges of the Christian life. The discussion questions provided will help you get going, but you will often find that it is in the discussions that follow *after* you have moved beyond the set questions in which you will find the greatest benefit.

There are numerous simple booklets available at your local Christian bookstore on how to lead a successful small group, and you are encouraged to study one if you feel the need. (A good one: *Leading Bible Discussions,* James Nyquist and Jack Kurhatschek, IV Press). For our purposes here, the following are some guidelines.

1. *Pray* for the right people to join the group and then approach those whom you feel best about inviting. Nine to twelve people is about as many as you will be able effectively to involve. Agree on the time, place, frequency of meetings, and length of meetings suitable to the group.

2. No two groups are alike. Some will have experienced believers familiar with scripture and with the concepts

in this book. Others will be new seekers. Some will jell easily with members willing to share personally; for others it will take time for some to speak out and to share personally. In some groups, prayer will be natural; in others it may be awkward at first.

3. Be sensitive to the needs of the group. Make each person feel important and comfortable. Be gentle and loving. Be flexible. Most importantly, pray for your group members daily throughout the study. Be in touch with them by phone. A leader's role is one of *encouragement*.

4. As the leader you will set the pattern for the others in your openness, your honesty, your acceptance of other viewpoints, and in your flexibility. Use the suggested questions as enablers to help the group talk openly about their response to the book, but don't be bound by these questions. You will often come up with other questions and ideas that will be even more suitable for your group.

5. Your group will gain much more in their discussions if the individuals have taken the time on their own, prior to the meetings, not just to have read the assigned chapter in advance, but also to have spent some time privately recording their own responses to the focus questions at the end of each chapter.

Have a wonderful time, and may God richly bless your group!

DISCUSSION QUESTIONS

INTRODUCTORY SESSION

1. Have a get-acquainted time in which each person in-
   troduces himself or herself. You might ask them to tell
   how long they have lived in the area, where they grew
   up, what their current life is like (single, married, em-
   ployment, family, hobbies, interests, church involve-
   ment, etc.).

2. Ask, "What is it about the life of Jesus that fascinates
   you the most and why?" Allow everyone to respond.

3. Give a brief description of the book. Assign chapter
   one to be read and the focus questions at the end of
   the chapter to be answered in advance of the meetings.

4. Have each person tell what they would like to get from
   this study. After reminding of time and place for the
   next meeting, close with prayer, asking one or more
   persons to pray and remember in prayer as many of
   the hopes expressed for the group as possible.

THE SECOND MEETING (After having read Chapter 1)

1. In any gathering there is likely to be someone whose
   own entrance into the world came about in notewor-
   thy circumstances. Ask members of the group to tell
   about the story of their own birth, noting anything unusual or specifically meaningful about it.

2. Are there any unique ways you or your family celebrate the birth of Jesus? Which customs or traditions

characteristic of your family are particularly meaningful to you?

3. Suppose we could go back in time and completely
   change how people in our country celebrate Christmas.
   What suggestions could you make as to some more appropriate ways we might celebrate the birth of God's
   son?

4. What do we really mean when we speak of spiritual
   birth? Can some in the group tell of a time in their
   own life when the Spirit of God first seemed to become
   real in their own life, when Christ became alive to
   them? What were some ways that spiritual growth
   soon followed spiritual birth?

5. What does a new Christian need in order to help him
   or her grow in Christian maturity?

6. What characteristics do we associate with spiritual infancy? You might refer to 1 Corinthians 3:1-4.

7. Infants are in need of certain special care. What special
   care does the spiritual infant need? How can we encourage one another's Christian growth in this group
   as we meet together regularly?

Perhaps, before closing, each person could express one
way in which they would like to grow or mature in their
Christian life. Draw the meeting to a close with prayer.

THE THIRD MEETING (After having read Chapter 2)

1. Read John 1:29-39. How do you suppose the followers
   of John would have felt as they observed the baptism
   of Jesus?

2. Has anyone a story to tell about their own baptism?
   Was there anything that marked it out as unusual or

especially notable? Or have someone share a recollection of a baptism they witnessed that was particularly meaningful, and tell why.

3. In this scene in the life of Jesus, we see the role of John as calling people to repent of their sins, while Jesus identifies himself with sinners by standing beside them. Why do we need both messages to come into a full relationship with God?

4. If baptism marks us out as belonging to God, how would you express some lessons you have learned in your own life about what it really means to belong to God? How does belonging to God change us (spiritually, intellectually, socially, emotionally, physically)?

5. Is there someone in the group who has experienced a time when they felt they did not belong to God? What happened? Have you learned something from this experience that might be worthwhile for the group to know? Romans 8:26-39 might be a helpful passage to read aloud.

6. What experiences, habits, or activities have helped us feel more completely secure in belonging to God? How might we help those we love to grow in their sense of belonging to God?

7. Perhaps there are concerns that someone in the group would like to express, so that as you close in prayer they might be remembered.

THE FOURTH MEETING (After having read Chapter 3)

1. Have members of the group tell something from their reading of Chapter 3 that they found to be especially significant and why.

2. Has someone had an experience of testing or tempta-

tion that eventually led to some kind of personal growth or helpful realization which they would be willing to tell the group?

3. The early Christians made much of the fact that Jesus was tempted in all the ways that we are and that, therefore, he understands clearly the difficulty we encounter in our own efforts to be fruitful for God. Would you rather take your troubles to someone who has been through the same sort of difficulties you are now going through, or someone who has not experienced such trials? How does this affect the way we pray? How honest can we be in our prayers? How should we feel about bringing our weaknesses or needs to Christ? (Matthew 11:28-30 contains an encouraging word in this regard.)

4. What do members of the group feel are some of the most common or frequent temptations that we face? Do these temptations have anything or any characteristics in common? What helps us to become stronger in the face of such temptations?

5. Remembering that the author described temptation as either a testing situation we are enduring or an enticement to wrong, ask the group members if they would like to share with the others a testing situation or any other sort of temptation they are encountering right now.

At the appropriate time to close, pray for the whole group and particularly for any who have shared in response to the last question.

THE FIFTH MEETING (After having read Chapter 4)

1. Sometimes we forget that God really does have the power to change lives. Ask members of the group to

recount some examples they have personally witnessed of how persons have been genuinely changed by a deepening relationship with our Lord.

2. For genuine, positive change to occur in a person's life, what factors, attitudes, or ingredients are most important for the person concerned? for friends and families?

3. Can someone in the group recount a personal example of genuine transformation in their own life—transformation of attitude? relationship? outlook? values? goals? To what do they attribute this change?

4. Why would we want to become more like Christ?

5. The process of becoming more like Christ is called sanctification. What do you feel are some of the most common barriers which hold people in your community back in their Christian growth?

6. Considering how Jesus himself dealt with a variety of individuals, how do you think the Lord would react to these various things that keep us from becoming wholly his? Discuss examples of people whom he encountered, as described in the gospels, for whom he had words of criticism. What attitudes did he seem to be seeking? What did people who experienced healing or dramatic change, through encounter with Jesus, have in common?

7. Ask the group members to express one area in their own lives in which they want to see the Holy Spirit help them to change, and then share in prayer for one another as you close.

THE SIXTH MEETING (After having read Chapter 5)

1. How do people in your circle of friends respond to

death? The death of others, and/or the prospect of their own death?

2. What do you think should be a Christian's attitude to death? Is this the common attitude you observe among your Christian friends? Why? Why not?

3. Could any in the group tell how they responded when they first really grasped the fact that Christ died for their sins? What was the impact or result of this realization? How has this made a difference in their lives since?

4. Is it harder to "die to selfishness" (the first death), or to die physically (the second death)? Which do you think is more important to God? Why? Can you "live for Christ" and live for self at the same time?

5. What have been some of the most important factors helping you learn more of what it means to live for Christ? Realizations? Hard lessons? Significant encounters? Books?

6. What are practical, simple ways we can help one another deal more effectively with sin in our own lives and encourage one another to know Christ?

Close in prayer as appropriate.

THE SEVENTH MEETING (After reading Chapter 6)

1. Ask the members of the group to share anything they have found interesting or helpful in the reading of Chapter 6.

2. Christians over the last several years have become more aware of the power of God at work in and through the lives of believers. Let us focus this discussion on some of the powerful ways the Holy Spirit is at

work in the church today. Tell of some ways that you have seen the power of God at work in answer to prayers, in healings, in seeing people's lives changed, in altering circumstances, etc.

3. Why are we hesitant to trust in the dynamic power of God's Spirit? Why are we sometimes reluctant to pray for God's power to work in certain situations?

4. Can someone tell of a situation that seemed absolutely impossible and overwhelming and yet, by God's grace and powerful help, resulted in wonderful changes coming about?

5. Is there some challenge that a member of the group is facing now that the group needs to commit to united prayer and to seeking God's powerful help or intervention?

Close in prayer as appropriate.

THE EIGHTH MEETING (After reading Chapter 7)

1. What are some of the implications of the ascension of Christ for Christ himself? For us?

2. What difference would it make if there had been no ascension of Christ?

3. What does it mean for us that Christ is the Lord of the universe?

4. What do you think the author meant towards the end of the chapter when he spoke of "looking down" rather than "being down"? How can we help each other to live "above" our circumstances rather than "under" our circumstances?

5. What are some of the subtle pressures that cause us to tend to look at things from our limited point of view,

rather than looking at them more from God's point of view? What can we do about this?

6. What do you think the atmosphere would be like in a church where many members were growing more and more in this sense of the "ascension" perspective? How can our church grow in this way? What can we as a group do to encourage spiritual renewal in our church or in our community?

Perhaps this last question should be the focus of prayer at this final meeting, and also a discussion of where you might want to go from here in terms of further meetings and further study projects.